What's Next in Your Life?

A Spiritual Guide to Retirement and Purposeful Aging

James I. Briggs

ISBN 979-8-89485-000-9 (Paperback)
ISBN 979-8-89485-001-6 (Digital)

Covenant Books
11661 Hwy 707
Murrells Inlet, SC 29576
www.covenantbooks.com

CONTENTS

Preface...v

Chapter 1: Setting the Stage: Some Initial Thoughts
            about Aging and Retirement 1
Chapter 2: Situating Yourself in the Aging Process and
            Beginning a Life Review.................................10
Chapter 3: Discerning What's Next in Your Life 21
Chapter 4: The Four Pillars of a Life Well Lived 31
Chapter 5: Exploring Identity, Meaning, and Purpose...............41
Chapter 6: Uncovering Your Deepest Desires...........................52
Chapter 7: Moving from Your Desires and Intentions
            to Action 58
Chapter 8: The Spiritual Dimension of Discerning
            Your Future..65
Chapter 9: Closing Thoughts on Aging and Retirement 82

Acknowledgments 85
Bibliography...89

PREFACE

At different times in our lives, we experience transitions from one life stage to another. The transition into retirement and the realization that we are growing older are two of those major transition points. Part of this transition is learning to accept the fact that we have lived more years than we have left to live. This realization can lead to a redefinition of what will give meaning and purpose to our lives as we go forward after leaving behind what was our life's work.

So much of our identity comes from the work we have done, the positions we have held, and the families we have raised. Shifting what defines our identity when we leave our profession or become an empty nester can be challenging and unsettling. This book includes a series of exercises that I and many others have done successfully to come to a clearer understanding of what we want to do next. That process can begin by answering three essential questions:

- How have you been gifted in life?
- To what purpose do you want to put those gifts at this point in your life?
- How can you be successful in achieving those purposes?

My personal interest in these topics arose from my work with men and women taking a sabbatical after many years of dedicated work in ministry. The demographic of this group was people in their sixties and seventies. One of the big questions they were asking was, What will I do next after my sabbatical? At this time, I was turning seventy and found myself motivated to understand more fully the aging process and the decision-making process around retirement, including how people make decisions about when to retire and what they want their retirement to look like personally.

After extensive reading (a bibliography of my favorite books on these topics can be found at the end of this book), I developed a short course to help folks answer these questions. The course then turned into workshops and retreats that I have been offering over the past eight years. This book reflects the lessons learned and the experiences shared by the groups of people that have come together to discern what's next in their lives.

As you will see, my approach is very much influenced by Ignatian spirituality that comes from my thirty years working at two Jesuit universities. Ignatian spirituality derives from the writings of St. Ignatius, especially his classic, *The Spiritual Exercises*. But you do not need to be a person of faith to participate in the reflective exercises I recommend. You can adapt them to your own experience without reference to any specific faith or spirituality. This book is meant to be a guide to self-reflection for all.

The exercises and questions I pose will open your mind and heart to a new way of thinking about and living this time in your life—call it retirement, semi-retirement, the second half of life, life's last third, the next chapter, whatever. I want to address the issues that inevitably come with growing older. But, most importantly, I want to inspire you to get in touch with your hopes and dreams for the rest of the wonderful gift of life you have been given post-retirement,

The outcome I desire for you is a more engaged, conscious living of a fuller life as you age—a life characterized by freedom rather than fear, gratitude rather than regret, and, ultimately, a deeper connection with the divine. This is a time of new beginnings built on an appreciation of God's abiding presence in your life and how God is calling you into this next stage of life.

The basic assumption of this book is that each of us is called and gifted by God; we spend a lifetime trying to hear that call ever more clearly. Hearing that call involves continually rediscovering who we are, what gifts we have been given, and the purpose to which we want to put those gifts in the service of others. We need all the help we can find to answer these questions and to hear the prompting of the Spirit. This book will hopefully provide some of that assistance.

This is not a book simply to be read. This book provides a framework and process for reflection. It includes a series of reflective exercises to help guide your thinking about that "what's next?" question. Give yourself the time and space you need with these exercises. By thoughtfully participating in these exercises, you can find the tools you need to develop a deeper understanding of the transition into retirement and greater clarity about what it is you want to do next with what the poet Mary Oliver calls *"your one wild and precious life?"*[1]

Happy reading and happy reflecting!

---

[1] From the poem "The Summer Day" by Mary Oliver (House of Light, Resource Press, 1990).

CHAPTER 1

SETTING THE STAGE: SOME INITIAL THOUGHTS ABOUT AGING AND RETIREMENT

If you are like me, you have mixed feelings about aging and retirement. We have things to look forward to and things that concern and worry us. To grapple with these mixed feelings, a good starting point is to write down your responses to the following two questions in our first reflective exercise:

REFLECTIVE EXERCISE NUMBER 1

What are the three things you are most looking forward to as you grow older in these post-retirement years? What do you see as the main blessings of growing older in the post-retirement years?

What are your three biggest concerns or worries about growing older? What do you see as the burdens of growing older?

Take some time writing your responses to these questions. When you are done with your own responses, compare your responses with those of others who have completed this exercise.

Among the more frequent responses to the question of what you are most looking forward to are these: more time with my family (spouse, children, and grandchildren) and friends, an increased commitment to some sort of community service, time to stay intellectually alive and learn some new things, pursuit of latent interests and hobbies, and the opportunity to travel to places I've always wanted to visit.

When it comes to worries and concerns, respondents frequently mentioned the following: diminished income; loss of professional identity; managing additional time with my spouse; assuming responsibility for the care of aging parents and maybe aging siblings; becoming ill myself, especially when it means losing my independence and becoming dependent on others for care; anticipating death—my own and those I know and love; and growing socially isolated.

The reality of growing older manifests itself in different ways— ways that I like to call wake-up calls. Here were a few of my personal wake-up calls: getting notices from AARP that I was now eligible for membership; eligibility for Medicare; standing on the BART train and being asked by someone if I would like to take their seat; turning seventy (that was thirteen years ago!); the increasing frequency of illness and death of family members and friends, including the death of my long-time boss, Paul Locatelli, SJ; my wife Kathy's recurring melanoma and the chemotherapy that helped save her life; the realization that I was now the oldest living member of my family on both my mother's and father's side; our four daughters having all turned forty and one almost ready to turn fifty! We all have our own wake-up calls—realizations that we are growing older, and we aren't as young as we used to be.

Reflect for a few moments on some of your own wake-up calls—messages that you are aging and that you are moving into a different or new stage of life. Make note of them.

The realization of growing older gives rise to what have been described as the three key concerns that come with aging. These three concerns are likely reflected in your own responses to the questions in the first reflective exercise above. Richard Bolles, in his book *What Color Is Your Parachute—In Retirement,* talks about these three:[2]

- *First, geo-financial. Will I have sufficient funds for the rest of my life? Will I outlive my resources?*

  Having financial stability and sufficient financial resources for the future is fundamental. This is probably why, when we hear advertisements about the importance of planning for retirement, the planning that is talked about is almost exclusively about financial planning.

  The financial resources needed will also depend, in large part, on where we want to live geographically. We want the home and the community environments that support the life we want to lead, but we need to be aware that the relative value of our money depends on *where* we are living, thus the reference to the *geo-financial* dimension of aging.

  The financial resources we will need depend, of course, on how long we will live and other factors, including our health. As a friend of mine so bluntly put it: "It would be a whole lot easier to plan for retirement if we only knew when we were going to die!"

  Financial planning is essential, but it is not the only dimension of our lives for which we need to plan.
- *Second, bio-medical.* Health is high on the list of concerns among those who are getting older. We need to work at maintaining good health and dealing successfully with health challenges that arise for our *physical* body. It is also essential that we have the best available health insurance we can afford, above and beyond our coverage under Medicare. In addition to access to quality health care, maintaining good health also requires attention to physical exercise and

---

[2] John E. Nelson and Richard N. Bolles, *What Color Is Your Parachute for Retirement* (Ten Speed Press, 2010).

sufficient rest. All of this contributes to our vitality, energy, strength, resilience, and endurance going forward.

- *Third, psychosocial and spiritual.* The psychosocial and spiritual dimension of our lives refers to our identity, the sense of who we are, and the meaning and purpose we give to our lives. The psychosocial refers to our relationships with others—family, friends, coworkers, and colleagues. The spiritual refers to our interior life and our relationship with the divine. This all adds up to a desire for a deeper sense of fulfillment and engagement in life for our *nonphysical* self.

While these three ingredients/elements/challenges are all important and all interconnected, it is this third dimension of aging—the psychosocial and spiritual dimensions of growing older—that will be the focus of what we will be discussing in the coming chapters. My assumptions are that you have a good degree of confidence that your financial resources will be sufficient for you, and that you are currently enjoying good overall health. Again I say this with the recognition that some diminishments are inevitable and part of the reality of aging.

Taking into account these three dimensions and using my experience working with people transitioning into this new stage of life, I have distilled the following seven essential elements of a good retirement and purposeful aging:

ESSENTIAL ELEMENTS OF A GOOD RETIREMENT/PURPOSEFUL AGING

- Steward your *financial resources* in ways that provide personal and familial financial security without undue worry or concern for the future. Also consider how your financial resources might be used to help meet the community/societal needs to which you commit yourself.
- *Work on being healthy.* Commit to physical exercise, good nutrition, and sufficient rest, and be sure you have the health insurance needed to cover both your anticipated and unanticipated health and medical needs.

- Stay *intellectually alive and stimulated.* Learn something new through reading, travel, short courses, hobbies like writing, painting, photography…and have fun.
- Take time to build, nourish, and rebuild *relationships with family and friends.* More deeply cherish those most dear to you—your spouse, your children and grandchildren, your extended family, and your friends.
- *Become engaged in service.* Find an opportunity to use your time, talents, and treasure to continue to make a difference in helping meet the needs of others.
- Carve out time for the *spiritual dimension of life* and decide how to infuse your life's choices with a sense of how God might be calling you, inviting you to action, and using your gifts in service of a purpose that continues to give meaning to your life as you grow older. Your relationship with God is foundational and provides clarity, focus, and perspective on the other elements of successful retirement and purposeful aging.
- Lastly, if you have a spouse or partner, make sure you are on the *same page as your spouse or partner* regarding your expectations, assumptions, hopes, and dreams for the years ahead. Maybe you could read this book at the same time and use it as a stimulus for conversation around your hopes and dreams for your lives together as you age. A very helpful resource for this conversation is *Loving Your Marriage in Retirement* by Sally Strosahl with contributions by Tom Johnson. Note especially her "Questions for Your Retirement Plan"!

This list is much like a recipe for a good soup. Each ingredient is important; however, it is in their combination and integration that the desired outcome is achieved.

Before moving on to helping you situate yourself on the spectrum of life stages and aging, let me say a few words about the word *retirement.* First, it is very important to recognize that the word carries negative connotations for many.

Leider and Shapiro, in their book *Claiming Your Place Around the Fire: Living the Second Half of Your Life on Purpose*, say this:

> For many people today, retirement is a roleless role. This is true in large part because the traditional notion of retirement fits with a worn-out notion of aging that conceives of it primarily in terms of disengagement and decline.[3]

Have you ever noticed how many words associated with retirement and aging begin with the letter *d?* Disengagement and decline quoted above are two of these words; here are some others: debilitation, deterioration, decrepitude, dependence, degeneration, dislocation, discontinuity, and deferral. Amazing, isn't it? Well, as we move forward, we will talk about substituting four *G* words for all these *D* words. The *G* words will be gift, gratitude, generosity, and generativity. More about these four pillars of a life well-lived in chapter 3.

The *D* words, however, do provide a gentle reminder that we need to recognize that there are struggles, suffering, and tragedies in life, and there are real diminishments that come with growing older. However, we must not let the reality of diminishment become life's dominant metaphor for aging.

My wife, Kathy, for example, refused for a long time to even use the word retirement because of some of the cultural connotations associated with it—your work is done; you are just going to take it easy and do nothing; you have nothing left to contribute; you're finished, done, cooked, over the hill.

Yet often I would come home to Kathy sitting on the couch and watching mind-numbing television for hours. I was worried. Who is this person? This was not the Kathy I knew—a person of energy, vibrancy, active engagement with others, and always making a positive contribution to the people and places where she worked. She explained to me that before taking on any new commitments in

---

[3]   Richard J. Leider and David A. Shapiro, *Claiming Your Place at the Fire: Living the Second Half of Your Life on Purpose* (Berrett-Koehler Publishers, Inc., 2004).

retirement, she thought it important to start by learning how to do nothing. Then only gradually would she make decisions about how she would use her gifts and spend her time in retirement.

I was reminded of this quote from, of all people, Winnie the Pooh: "*Doing nothing often leads to the very best something.*" That has been true for Kathy, as she has found a beautiful balance in her life—volunteering at the county hospital, helping at our church, reading voraciously, and having the availability for the two of us to spend precious time with our family, especially our twelve grandchildren.

Kathy has also taught me how important it is for each of us to define retirement in our own very personal way, rethinking, reimagining our lives and what will give us meaning and purpose as we age.

In our culture, negative and stultifying stereotypes and the worship of youthfulness can be very dispiriting. Advertising tells us constantly how we can fight against the aging process. Aging is seen as a period of decline—maybe in the form of mental and/or physical diminishment. Aging is often seen as a time when we lose value and respect. We can feel *invisible* in conversations and ignored as *irrelevant*. How different this is from the notion of "*elder*" in other cultures and traditions, including Native American, African, and Jewish, where the wisdom and experience of those who are older are sought after and highly valued and respected. This invisibility and irrelevancy also cause many of us to struggle anew with the question of meaning and purpose in our lives.

Louise Aronson, in her book *Elderhood*, makes this important observation:

> If we pander to prejudice about aging, we should not be surprised to find ourselves invisible, overlooked, or discarded. Rather older people should be offered a world view that says to them: We still see you and we still like, love, respect, admire and are inspired by you, both for who you were AND for who you are, a person completing the full arc of human life. (Aronson, *Elderhood*)

So it is up to each one of us to counter the cultural stereotypes about aging and retirement. Some have even suggested some new variations on the word retirement to counter its negative connotations. Here are a few of them: re-wirement, re-firement, re-aspirement, and re-desirement. The intent here is to overcome some of the negative stereotypes associated with retirement and emphasize its positive dimensions.

Here's a favorite quote of mine from Joan Chittister, probably my favorite author on the subject of growing older. Her words capture the essence of conscious, purposeful aging and retirement:

> These later years are gift, not burden…The task of this stage of life is not simply to endure the coming end of time, it is to come alive in ways I have never been alive before. (Chittister, *The Gift of Years*)

Despite some of the messages in our culture that the elderly are out of touch, no longer of use, and of little value, the exercises in this book are intended to keep us focused on the positive—that retirement and aging are about new beginnings, and we must each decide what we want to make of our retirement and our remaining years.

Let me close this chapter with one of my favorite poems by the Irish poet John O'Donohue:

For a New Beginning

In out-of-the-way places of the heart,
Where your thoughts never think to wander,
This beginning has been quietly forming,
Waiting until you were ready to emerge.

For a long time, it has watched your desire,
Feeling the emptiness growing inside you,
Noticing how you willed yourself on,
Still unable to leave what you had outgrown.

It watched you play with the seduction of safety
And the gray promises that sameness whispered,
Heard the waves of turmoil rise and relent,
Wondered would you always live like this.

Then the delight, when your courage kindled,
And out you stepped onto new ground,
Your eyes young again with energy and dream,
A path of plenitude opening before you.

Though your destination is not yet clear
You can trust the promise of this opening.
Unfurl yourself into the grace of beginning
That is at one with your life's desire.

Awaken your spirit to adventure;
Hold nothing back, learn to find ease in risk;
Soon you will home in a new rhythm,
For your soul senses the world that awaits you.

With this bit of background, let us now move into the first step in our process of discerning what's next in your life—situating yourselves in the aging process.

CHAPTER 2

SITUATING YOURSELF IN THE AGING PROCESS AND BEGINNING A LIFE REVIEW

In coming to a deeper understanding of your aging, it is helpful to situate yourself in the aging process. In doing this, it is important to understand the changing demographics of aging and the dramatic increase in the lifespan of the population of the United States. The upward trend in longevity has opened a whole range of challenges and opportunities unknown and unavailable to the earlier generations that have preceded us.

In 1900, 40 percent of the population was under seventeen, and only 4 percent was over sixty-five. Now, in the United States, 55.8 million adults are aged sixty-five and older, accounting for about 17 percent of the nation's population. By 2040, that proportion is projected to grow to 22 percent, to over 80 million people[4] (Institute on Aging, San Francisco, California).

This has prompted insurance companies to increase their projected life expectancy for planning purposes. For example, TIAA CREF has moved life expectancy from ninety-seven to ninety-nine to ensure sufficient coverage for its policyholders.

Here's another interesting statistic: If you live to eighty-five, on average, you will live another seven years to ninety-two!

---

[4] Institute on Aging (San Francisco, CA).

With the period of midlife becoming extended, some have suggested a new life stage be added to the traditional stages of life we learned in our psychology classes. The following diagram illustrates the naming and positioning of this new life stage:

Stages of Life/Human Development

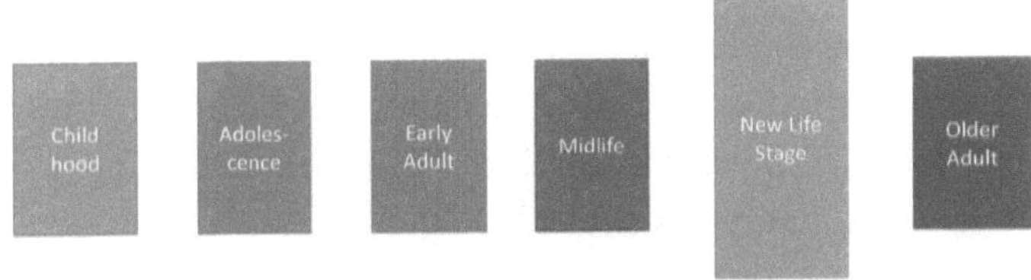

In their book *Claiming Your Place at the Fire: Living the Second Half of Your Life on Purpose,* Leider and Shapiro say this about our increased longevity:

> New elders today have a lot more time to age before they become elderly. With that time, we believe that their biggest personal challenge will be to re-invent themselves for what longevity could mean.[5] (Leider/Shapiro, 135)

Joan Chittister, in her book *The Gift of Years*, puts it this way:

> Later life is largely our own creation... Diminishment is no longer the principal characteristic of aging. On the contrary, we are now developing in ways that only a short time ago would have been considered impossible for anyone over the age of forty.[6] (Chittister)]

---

[5] Richard Leider and David Shapiro, *Claiming Your Place at the Fire* (Berrett-Koehler, 2004).

[6] Joan Chittister, *The Gift of Years: Growing Older Gracefully* (Blue Bridge, 2008, 2014).

However, despite decades of increases in longevity, in 2018, the Centers for Disease Control and Prevention announced that the lifespan of the average American had declined for the third consecutive year. The tipping point was in 2015, the first year of decline since World War II. The decline was attributed to the opioid crisis and increased suicide rates. But the most dramatic declines have occurred in the last several years, with COVID-19 deaths added to those from opioid overdoses, suicides, homicides, and accidental deaths.

The Centers for Disease Control's National Center for Health Statistics shows that, as a result, life expectancy dropped from 78.8 years in 2019 to 77.3 years in 2020 to 76.4 years in 2022—a drop of almost two and a half years since 2019.

As important and interesting as these changing demographics are on a national level, they may or may not have an impact on our own individual aging and longevity. What is most important is facing and acknowledging our own individual paths of aging. To help promote your reflection on your own personal reality of aging, I would like you to complete what I call the 80 Box Exercise. Here are the eighty boxes:

Each of these eighty boxes represents a year of your life. So, with your chart oriented horizontally, I ask you to start in the upper left-hand corner and moving left to right, mark an *x* in each of the boxes moving down the chart until you have marked the number of boxes that total your current age. Each row of ten boxes represents a decade of your life. For those of you over eighty, add another row of ten boxes along the bottom of the chart to have a box for each year you have lived. Take some time to complete this exercise now.

When you have completed this and have an *x* in every box you have lived, take a few minutes to jot down some notes on any feelings that may have surfaced as you did this exercise.

What feelings does this exercise evoke when you realize how many years you already lived? And how many years you may have left to live?

This 80 Box Exercise was introduced to me over dinner by one of my closest friends. My initial reaction after completing the exercise was that it visibly drove home for me the reality of my own aging. I clearly remember my response to him after completing the exercise. I said sarcastically, "Well, thanks a lot for this!" I was basically saying I didn't appreciate his effort to remind me of the reality that I was growing older.

There are different possible reactions or feelings we might have about completing this exercise. For some, it evokes feelings of gratitude for all the years lived. For others, it brings back memories of challenging or sorrowful times in their lives, as well as life's successes and high points. For others, it surfaces some of the fears and anxieties they may have about growing older. Others talk about an increased sense of urgency, knowing the time they may have left is limited.

Wendy Lustbader, in her book *Life Gets Better—The Unexpected Pleasures of Growing Older*, captures the sense of urgency with these words:

> The shock of realizing we have gotten older
> often turns *someday* into *now.* We suddenly locate
> ourselves further on the trajectory between birth
> and death, and a bolder spirit overtakes us…

> Something spurs us to recognize that our former **purposes** do not suffice, and we cannot wait any longer to follow our heart's desire…
>
> The energy of finitude impels us to speak what is true for us and act on our deepest **purposes**.[7] (Lustbader; emphasis added)

It is the word purpose that is so important. Redefining and reimagining our purpose as we leave our careers behind is key to a good retirement and purposeful aging. We will talk more about this in chapter 4.

To temper this sense of urgency, Lustbader goes on to say:

> When life's end seems nearer, a lifetime of rushing around and striving to get to my next goal may subside into appreciation for what is right in front of us. If we let it, scarcity of time ahead breeds attentiveness to the present moment. (Lustbader)

One of my favorite Zen sayings provides a different perspective on the urgency we may feel because we are growing older:

> We have to slow down because we do not have much time.

So what is clear to us from the 80 Box Exercise is that we are growing older. The question is what we are going to do about this realization. Let me share with you two of my other favorite quotes on aging:

> Aging is beyond our control but how we age is up to us. (Lewis Richmond, *Aging as a Spiritual Practice*)

---

[7] Wendy Lustbader, *Life Gets Better: The Unexpected Pleasures of Growing Older* (Penguin Group, 2011).

It is not how old we are, but how we are old.
(Jules Renard)

What I find stimulating about these perspectives is that they all speak to the issue of agency. In other words, what am I going to do with this realization that I am growing older? What will be my attitude toward aging? How will I choose to live my life? If I have more time behind me than ahead of me, how do I best use the time remaining? In other words, time becomes more meaningful. Now it is simply time to spend time well, savoring every moment.

But before we start planning for what's ahead, it is important to review our past and look for themes that may help us clarify our future direction. That brings us to our next reflective exercise—a life review by decade. Building on the simple 80 Box Exercise you have already completed, use this as an in-depth tool to review and remember your personal history and experiences. This process is called a life review. It is essential to the process of moving from where we have been in our lives to moving forward into this next stage of our lives. Take your time with this. Even though it may take several hours, I guarantee it will be time well spent!

REFLECTIVE EXERCISE NUMBER 2
LIFE REVIEW BY DECADE

Use this exercise for a deeper review of your life by each decade you have lived, reflecting on the following questions (perhaps develop a format or chart for this exercise):

- *For each decade already lived, what was your primary role during that time?*
- *What were the key accomplishments/blessings of each decade?*
- *What major decisions/key transitions were made during these times?*
- *Was there some challenge, suffering, or loss during this time?*
- *Who were the key people accompanying you, supporting you, or advising you at this time in your life?*

- *Did faith play a role in the decisions you were making and the path you were following?*

After using the above questions to reflect on each decade of your life, review your responses and ask yourself these final questions:

> *What connections can you make between your life already lived and your life yet to be lived? Is there a thread or a theme that connects all the parts of your life?*

I want to emphasize the importance of determining whether there is a thread or theme that connects all the parts of your life or which surfaces as a key to who you are and what you want your life to mean. I love the concept of "thread' and have been amazed at the frequency of references to the notion of a life thread among a number of important authors.

Here are some quotes that capture the idea of identifying the way your experiences are connected to each other and to your individuality.

Arthur Schopenhauer, a German metaphysician from the nineteenth century, provides an image that is very helpful. He said:

> We spend our early years weaving the fabric of our lives. There comes a point when it is time to turn over the fabric and see how the threads are connected.

St. Teresa of Avila, from sixteenth-century Spain, put it this way:

> The love of God weaves the disparate fragments of life into a tapestry of wholeness and holiness.

And the contemporary writer, Parker Palmer, captures his experience this way:

> Looking back, I see why I needed the tedium and the inspiration, the anger and the love, the anguish and the joy. I see how it all belongs... Calamities I once lamented now appear as strong threads of a larger weave, without which the fabric of my life would be less resilient.[8]

But perhaps the most substantive reflection on the notion of "thread," comes from William Stafford in his book *The Way It Is*:

> There's a thread you follow. It goes among things that change. But it doesn't change. People wonder about what you are pursuing. You have to explain about the thread. But it is hard for others to see. While you hold it, you can't get lost. Tragedies happen; people get hurt or die, and you suffer and get old. Nothing you do can stop time's unfolding. But you don't ever let go of the thread.[9]

So now you can see the importance of life review to our process. David Brooks, commentator and author of his book entitled *The Second Mountain*, puts it this way:

> One task in life is synthesis. It is to collect all the fragmented pieces of a self and bring them to a state of unity, so that you can move coherently toward a single vision.[10]

---

[8] Parker Palmer, *On the Brink of Everything: Grace, Gravity, and Getting Old* (Berrett-Koehler Publishers, Inc., 2018).

[9] William Stafford, *The Way It Is* (Graywolf Publishing, 1999).

[10] David Brooks, *The Second Mountain: The Quest for a Moral Life* (Random House, 2019).

Brooks quotes Friedrich Nietzsche:

> The way you discover what you were put on earth for is to go back into your past, list the times you were fulfilled, and then see if you can draw a line through them to connect them.

That line referenced by Nietzsche is the thread Stafford is talking about! That line, that thread, can give you a very strong hint about where the meaning and purpose of your life lie.

As you process your work on Reflective Exercise Number 2, you should feel a deep sense of gratitude for the gift of time you have been given and for all the blessings of your life. You may also come to appreciate that, in retrospect, some of the burdens you may have experienced in your life have turned out to be blessings in disguise. For me, this has led to a deeper appreciation of God's providence. In my favorite definition of God's providence, it is described as God's caring provision for his people as he guides them in their journey of faith through life, accomplishing his purpose in them. I believe this to be true. Even for the nonbelievers, this exercise can help identify how difficult situations often lead to positive outcomes.

However, I also realize that what is most providential are the many people who have an important influence on our lives. One of the most important questions in the life review exercise references the people who have stood by us and helped guide us through the significant milestones and transitions in our lives.

I first reflected on this question during a retreat I was privileged to make at Mepkin Abbey outside of Charleston, South Carolina. On the grounds of this Trappist abbey is a huge labyrinth carved out of a cornfield. I decided I was going to envision each turn in the labyrinth as a turning point or transition in my life and call to mind the people who were standing by me during each transition. When I came to the end of the labyrinth, on the benches around the circular clearing in the center of the labyrinth sat all the people whom I had called to mind and thanked for their roles in my life. I am not a person prone to mystical experiences, but this was a big one. It reminded me again of the words of Joan Chittister:

> When we find ourselves alone, enjoying our solitude, all the people we have ever known, still very much alive in us, come back again to help us see where we have been, to understand what (and whom) we have become, to help us chart what it will take to make these final years our best ones.

And so look back over the way you have come and ask what has been and will be the essence of your life. A first step in this process is to count your blessings and to call to mind all the ways you have been gifted and blessed in your life. This is the starting point from which you can build the four pillars of a well-lived life.

REFLECTIVE EXERCISE NUMBER 3

Create a list of all the ways you have been gifted and blessed in your life up to this point, all the things in your life for which you are thankful, and all your reasons to be grateful. Be sure to include among your gifts such things as the special people in your life—family, friends, teachers, bosses, etc.; educational opportunities; work experiences and accomplishments; travel opportunities, etc.

For those of you who have a vibrant prayer life, you may want to consider this list a litany, putting your gifts and blessings in prayer form like this: For…, I give you thanks, O God.

A closing prayer to which we can all relate as we end this chapter:

> We ask you, loving God, to give each one of us an intimate knowledge of the many gifts we have received. Filled with gratitude for all of them, may we in all things return God's gift of love through our own lives of loving, serving, and building God's kingdom.

Loving God, teach me this one thing above all: what are my choices, and how do I discover the freedom you call me to so that I can return to you all the wonders and gifts you have poured out on me. Let me be aware of the hope you find within me so that I may be true to myself as you call me into the next phase of my life.

Father, guide us in choosing how to live our lives more and more with and in your Son, Jesus Christ, and in response to the promptings of the Holy Spirit. Amen.

CHAPTER 3

DISCERNING WHAT'S NEXT IN YOUR LIFE

Having spent some time working toward the completion of Reflective Exercises Number 2 and Number 3, you have begun the process of discerning your future. So, before going any further in the process, it is important to know what it means to discern. Discernment is not merely a human discipline. It is not just a matter of rational decision-making. Discernment adds a spiritual dimension to the rational process, and that spiritual dimension connects your desires with your perception of what God desires for you.

The foundation of discernment is recognition and awareness of the presence and action of a loving God in our past and in the present moment. So, when we discern, we are attempting to reconcile and align our desires with God's desires for us.

This affects the framing of some of the questions that are key to our coming to greater clarity about our identity and what we want to do next in our lives. For example:

- Who am I in God's eyes?
- For what was I created?
- For what am I even now being created?
- When have I been most perfectly aligned with my calling?
- To what might God be calling me now, at this stage of my life?

Questions such as these open the door to what it means to discern. In my study of discernment, I have compiled some of my favorite definitions of discernment. These might be helpful to your own understanding of this process:

- That imperfect and sometimes wonderful process of finding clarity about God's leading; developing an inner confidence in God's leading.
- A framework that enables us to join in partnership with God in making choices that will help to bring about the fulfillment of God's generous hopes and desires—for the world and for us.
- The art of listening to our inner selves and learning to distinguish movements that arise from the Holy Spirit (our true, authentic selves) from those that do not.
- The foundation of discernment is recognition and awareness of the presence and action of a loving God in our past, in the present moment, and as we find our way forward into the future.

So when we talk about discernment, or discerning the life and work to which God is calling us, it involves both

- listening to ourselves, exploring our deepest desires, assessing *what we have to offer and the purpose to which we want to put what we have to offer*—these are the two key questions to answer—and
- listening to the promptings of the Holy Spirit as we answer these questions.

Here's a visual you might find helpful:

Key Questions

These questions are deeply rooted in Ignatian spirituality. They are embedded in these remarkable words of St. Ignatius talking about the nature of our calling:

> In calling me to live my **special qualities and characteristics,** God planted deep in myself an original **purpose**—what my concrete self adds up to—and the desire to live that out.

He goes on to say:

> There are very few people who realize what God would make of them...if they abandoned themselves into his hands and let themselves be formed by his grace.

Thomas Merton adds some helpful words about discerning our calling:

> Discovering vocation does not mean scrambling toward some prize just beyond my reach but accepting the treasure of true self I already possess... Vocation does not come from a voice

"out there" calling me to be something I am not. It comes from a voice "in here" calling me to be the person I was born to be, to fulfill the original selfhood given me at birth by God… Finally I am coming to the conclusion that my highest ambition is to be what I already am. That I will never fulfill my obligation to surpass myself unless I first accept myself, and if I accept myself fully in the right way, I will already have surpassed myself.

These two quotes, one from St. Ignatius and the other from Thomas Merton, point out the importance of self-knowledge, self-acceptance, and God's acceptance and love of us, unconditionally, with all our positives as well as our negatives.

The spiritual writer Ron Rolheiser, in his book *Sacred Fire*, captures it this way:

> To the extent I find my deepest identity, the closer I come to the God who created me and who lives within me.[11]

So how do we come to this deeper sense of our own identity and our own giftedness? We can come to a deeper self-understanding first by looking backward over our lives and doing a life review such as was suggested in the Reflective Exercise in chapter 2. You will also find it helpful to ponder and respond in writing to the questions posed in the next Reflective Exercise.

---

[11] Ron Rolheiser, *Sacred Fire* (Image, 2014).

REFLECTIVE EXERCISE NUMBER 4
DISCERNING YOUR CALLING

As the next step in your discernment process, reflect on the following questions related to discerning your calling and put your responses in writing:

- *When have I been happiest in terms of my effectiveness and productivity? In terms of the alignment of my work with Gospel values?*
- *What do I dream of in my life going forward that will create a more whole and balanced me?*
- *What is it that I feel I am being called to next in my life—in my relationships with family and friends, with God, and in my service to community?*
- *How do I see my gifts, talents, and desires connecting with the needs (personal and societal) I am most drawn to addressing at this stage of my life?*

For me, the following good advice from St. Teresa of Avila really hits home when it comes to connecting our individual giftedness with the needs we see around us:

May we struggle with the way our sense of our personal life calling relates to the **needs** of the world and our sense of hope for all people, across the street, around town, and around the world.

May we anchor our decisions in the hope of participating in life-giving ways to **areas of need** in our communities and the world.

So, as we go through this process of discernment, what must we do to properly discern? Here are several fundamental requirements of good discernment:

- A daily, living relationship with God is a precondition for good discernment; finding times of silent listening to hear the voice of God.
- Paying attention to the signs and experiences that let you know when God is stirring within you.
- Hearing God's callings as they manifest themselves in your temperament, talents, and intellectual capacities and in your aspirations and desires.
- Being pulled by grace toward God's will—to accept with a generous spirit whatever it is that God regards as best for you.
- Being open in mind and heart to hearing God say something different from what you expected.
- Focusing on God in the midst of our daily living and working, not just at the time of major decisions in our lives.

Similarly, at the beginning of the *Spiritual Exercises*, Ignatius spells out seven basic attitudes or qualities that a person must have as preconditions for entering into an authentic discernment process seeking God's will. These are outlined by David Fleming, SJ, in his book *Draw Me Into Your Friendship: The Spiritual Exercises, a Literal Translation and a Contemporary Reading*. They are the following:

1. *Openness.* We must approach the decision in question with an open mind and an open heart.
2. *Generosity.* To enter into a decision-making process with such openness requires a generous spirit with which we, with a largeness of heart, put no conditions on what God might call us to.
3. *Courage.* Such openness and generosity require courage, for God might be asking something different, challenging, and risky of us. It takes courage to give up control and trust-

ingly put the decision in God's hands while seeking God's will over our own.

4. *Interior freedom.* To make such a prayerful, generous, and courageous decision requires interior freedom. This means our whole and deepest desire is to do whatever God's will is for us, with no conditions attached. This is the attitude necessary to authentically find and follow God's will for us.

5. *A habit of prayerful reflection on one's experience.* How can we hear God's call if we're not listening? How can we listen if we're not praying? To make a prayerful decision, we must first pray, putting aside a significant portion of time (twenty minutes or more) on a daily basis to quiet ourselves, put ourselves in God's presence, and listen to what God is saying to us in the interior of our hearts.

6. *Having one's priorities straight.* There is a ruthless logic to Ignatius's spirituality. If serving God, our Creator and Lord, is the ultimate goal of our lives, then everything else in our lives must be kept in the subordinate position of a means to that end. This means that things such as opportunities, experiences, and relationships are to be valued and chosen only insofar as they contribute to our ultimate goal in life and rejected insofar as they deter us from that goal.

7. *Not confusing ends with means.* Ignatius comments: "It becomes obvious how easy it is for me to forget such a simple truth as the end and goal of my whole existence when I consider the manner in which choices are often made."

For St. Ignatius, discernment is a process for making choices in a context of faith, when the option is not between good and evil but between several possible courses of action, all of which are potentially good.

In pursuing the discernment process, he urges honest attention not only to the rational (reasons pro and con) but also to the realm of one's feelings, emotions, and desires—what Ignatius called "movements" of soul. A fundamental question in discernment becomes, "Where is this impulse from—the good spirit (of God) or the evil spirit (leading one away from God)?" A key to answering this question, says Ignatius in his *Spiritual Exercises*, is that, in the case of a person leading a basically good life, the good spirit gives "consolation"—the good spirit acts quietly and gently and leads one to peace, joy, and deeds of loving service—while the bad spirit brings "desolation." The bad spirit agitates, disturbs the peace, and injects fears and discouragement to keep one from doing good.

THREE MOVEMENTS IN DISCERNMENT

- *Be attentive* to what is happening in and around you (*see*).
- *Be reflective* about what you are attentive to (*judge*).
- *Be generous* (*decide, act*).

As we discern, what we hope for is greater clarity around the decisions we make for our future. So how will we experience this clarity and feel that sense of consolation Ignatius speaks of? Some positive signs of clarity include the following:

- We have a sense of congruence, of integration, and of alignment between our sense of self and the divine.
- The movement toward a decision comes from within, from our deep longing and desiring.
- We feel a new sense of energy—psychic, physical, and spiritual.
- We sense a readiness and resolve to take action, moving from desire to intention to action as we live out our deepest desires with boldness and courage!

So much of our discernment is related to uncovering our aspirations for the future and the kind of life we want for ourselves in our retirement years. St. Teresa of Avila has some inspiring words in this regard:

> It is a great help in our quest to have high
> aspirations, because often our actions begin with

our thoughts and our dreams. It is not pride to have great desires. It is the devil who makes us think that the lives of the saints are to be admired but not imitated…

Like the saints we need to be humble but bold in our pursuit, trusting God and not ourselves. For our Lord loves and seeks courageous souls.

Let us not fail to reach our destiny because we have been too timid, too cautious in our desires, because we sought too little.

It is true that I might stumble for trying to do too much too soon, but it is certain that I will never succeed if I hope for too little or, out of fear of failing, start not at all.

Pedro Arrupe, past superior general of the Society of Jesus, gives us further encouragement to use our imaginations in our discernment:

Nothing is more practical than finding God, that is in falling in love in a quite absolute, final way. What seizes your imagination will affect everything. It will decide everything. It will decide what gets you out of bed in the morning, what you do with your evenings, how you spend your weekends, what you read, whom you know, what breaks your heart, and what amazes you with joy and gratitude.

No matter how many years you have left, be inspired to get in touch with your hopes and your dreams for the rest of the wonderful gift of life you have been given.

If you feel the need for a deeper understanding of discernment and the challenges it entails, I highly recommend a book by Stefan Kiechle, SJ, entitled *The Art of Discernment*. Kiechle provides some very good practical considerations of how to notice and work through issues that arise when one makes an important decision.

And so we close this chapter with a prayer for the success of our discernment:

A Discerner's Prayer

God has called each of us by name. God has apportioned to each of us many strengths and abilities and surrounds us with people to love. His favor lies with each of us. Our lives are God's gift to us, and our lives are our response to God's gifts. God comes to us disguised as our lives so may we live our lives to the full.

Holy One, you are the Good Shepherd who fills the hungry with good things, who spreads a table before us, who fills our cups to overflowing, who calls each of us by name and leads us out. Thank you for all your gifts.

Today I am seeking to discern those special gifts you have given me to make me a channel of your love for others and to use those gifts to help build your kingdom.

Open my eyes to your ways. Tune my ears to your voice. Teach me what is important for me to know right now as I reflect on who I am and the meaning of my life.

Amen.

CHAPTER 4

THE FOUR PILLARS OF A LIFE WELL LIVED

There are four pillars of a life well lived—gift, gratitude, generosity, and generativity—four words starting with *G*, so they are easy to remember and are a counter force to all the *d* words associated with aging talked about in chapter 1. These pillars form the foundation of our approach to retirement and purposeful aging.

The first pillar is *gift*. If you are a person of faith, the place to begin is with God's *gift* of unconditional love for us individually, personally. God takes the initiative; God first loves us—freely, unconditionally, and deeply.

> *In this is love, not that we loved God but that*
> *God loved us. We love God because God first loved*
> *us. (1 John 4:10, 19)*

We call to mind all the ways that God has graced and blessed our lives. We think of family and friends. We think of the opportunities we have been given to develop and demonstrate our knowledge, skills, abilities, and personal qualities and to share our experience and wisdom with others. We think of all the wonders of nature and the universe. The list can go on and on; even our challenges can be gifts and blessings.

You have begun to capture your own gifts and blessings in Reflective Exercise Number 3. Keep this list going; it can go on and on, and remember that even our challenges and setbacks can turn into gifts and blessings.

More specifically, I suggest you also take some time to focus on your personal giftedness—the knowledge, skills, abilities, and personal qualities you bring to the world. Sometimes we need some assistance in identifying and validating our own giftedness. That may be because we lack the language to capture our giftedness, or it may be because some of those gifts and talents come so easily to us that we don't recognize them as special strengths of ours. Here's an exercise to help identify your giftedness and clarify what it is you have to offer others in terms of that giftedness.

REFLECTIVE EXERCISE NUMBER 5

Think back on your life and pick out what, for you, are three of your most rewarding experiences. They might include a personal contribution you made to your work or a few of your most important achievements or accomplishments. Jot down a few notes about each of these three experiences—when was it; where were you and with whom were you working; what was it that you accomplished that was so rewarding; what did you bring to the experience (knowledge, skills, personal qualities) that resulted in the positive outcome. Evaluate each of these experiences according to three dimensions:

1. *Skills and abilities. Thoroughly describe in detail three peak moments/accomplishments from your career. Reflecting on your three peak moments/accomplishments, identify the skills and personal qualities you manifested in each of these situations. When finished, reflect on your life experience in general and identify other skills that are your strongest and those you enjoy using the most. Go back over the lists and rank the level of skill you possess in each area you have marked. Also consider using these two online skill identification tools: Richard Bolles's Skill List at https://careergrow.coach/wp-content/uploads/2016/09/Bolles-Skills-List.pdf and the Clifton Strengths Assessment at https://www.gallup.com/cliftonstrengths.*

2. *Personal qualities/character strengths. Personal strengths are the attributes, activities, or tasks you excel at. For example, think about characteristic traits like being sociable, charismatic, or open-minded. We can conceive of character strengths as the ways and means we use to express our values and strive toward the virtues we find most meaningful. For help identifying your top five character strengths, use the questionnaire, VIA Signature Strengths, at www.authentichappiness.com.*

3. *Values. Get in touch with the values that guide and inspire how you live your life. Personal values are a set of guiding principles and beliefs that help you differentiate between "good" and "bad." Personal values influence your behaviors, relationships, and everyday life. They guide you through important decision-making and influence your personal development. Everyone prioritizes their core values differently, and yours shape how you uniquely move through the world. For help in clarifying your values, go to: www.therapistaid.com/therapy-worksheet/values-clarification. Use your core values to help discern the meaning and purpose of your life going forward.*

The second pillar is *gratitude*—our natural human response to the gifts we have received and to all the ways God loves us, blesses us, and gifts us.

We express our deep thanks for the gift of God's loving presence in our lives and for all that God is, has done, and means in our lives.

Consider these three beautiful quotes about gratitude:

- Dietrich Bonhoeffer: "Gratitude is the first movement of the spiritual life. It is a virtue to be practiced, it is a way of prayer."
- Anthony De Mello: "As we express our gratitude, we sanctify all the things for which we are thankful."
- Meister Eckhart, an eighteenth-century German Dominican mystic: "If the only prayer you say in your entire life is thank you, it will be enough."

While Eckhart's words convey a beautiful sentiment and emphasize the importance of gratitude, it leads us to consider whether gratitude is enough or if part of its value is in how it leads us to question what we can give back in return for the many gifts and blessings we have received. Is gratitude enough, or are we led to something more? Gratitude always seems to lead to the question of what I can give back in return for all the ways that I have been gifted and blessed.

In other words, *gratitude begets generosity*, the third pillar. A true mark of gratitude is our desire to give something to others in return for all that has been given to us.

To quote Pope Francis: *"For if we have received the love that restores meaning to our lives, how can we fail to share that love with others?"*

Wendy Lustbader says this: "Most of us become convinced over time that the spirit for a life well-lived derives from what we give to others, not what we amass for ourselves... We find there is strength in doing what good we can for others, not as an intellectual construct but as a way of meeting each day" (Lustbader, *Life Gets Better*). In other words, how will I, with a generous heart, share the love, mercy, and compassion that I have received from God and others?

To quote Pope Francis again: *"Our invitation to receive God's love and to love him in return, brings forth in our lives and actions a primary and fundamental response—to desire, seek, and protect the good of others."*

"When people make **generosity** part of their daily routine, they re-fashion who they are... The people who radiate a permanent joy have given themselves over to lives of deep and loving commitment. Giving has become their nature, and little by little they have made their souls incandescent" (David Brooks, *Second Mountain*, xxxi).

Ultimately, it is not just about our relationship with God; it is about generosity and generativity and how we return God's love to us through our love of neighbor. In the words of Pope Francis: "Works of love directed toward one's neighbor are the most perfect manifestation of the interior grace of the Spirit."

Bishop Robert Barron puts it this way:

> In its essence, love is an act of will—more precisely, the willing of the good of the other as other. To love is really to want what is good for someone else and then to act on that desire... Real love is leaping outside of the narrow confines of my needs and desires. It embraces the good of the other for the other's sake. It is an escape from the black hole of the ego, which rends to draw everything around it into itself.

So, as we move into this next stage of our lives, these are the key questions we need to answer: How have I been gifted, and how will I give back for all the ways I have been gifted and blessed in my life? In other words, how will I use my gifts to meet a need/serve a purpose?

We can take reassurance that these are the right questions, in part because of their connections to both Scripture and to a key section of the *Spiritual Exercises* of St. Ignatius. Consider first these words of St. Paul in the First Letter to the Corinthians 12:4–11:

> Now there are varieties of gifts, but the same Spirit; and there are varieties of service, but the same Lord; and there are varieties of activities, but it is the same God who empowers them all in everyone. To each is given the manifestation of the Spirit for the common good. For to one is given through the Spirit the utterance of wisdom, and to another the utterance of knowledge according to the same Spirit, to another faith by the same Spirit, to another gifts of healing by the one Spirit, to another the working of miracles, to another prophecy, to another the ability to distinguish between spirits, to another various kinds of tongues, to another the interpretation of tongues. All these are empowered by one and the

same Spirit, who apportions to each one individually as he wills. (1 Cor 12:4–11)

And then, in verses 12–26, Paul goes on to say:

> For just as the body is one and has many members, and all the members of the body, though many, are one body, so it is with Christ. For in one Spirit we were all baptized into one body Jews or Greeks, slaves or free and all were made to drink of one Spirit. For the body does not consist of one member but of many. If the foot should say, "Because I am not a hand, I do not belong to the body," that would not make it any less a part of the body. And if the ear should say, "Because I am not an eye, I do not belong to the body," that would not make it any less a part of the body. If the whole body were an eye, where would be the sense of hearing? If the whole body were an ear, where would be the sense of smell? But as it is, God arranged the members in the body, each one of them, as he chose. If all were a single member, where would the body be? As it is, there are many parts, yet one body.

Here's how St. Ignatius sums it up in section number 233 of *The Spiritual Exercises*:

> I ask God to give me an **intimate knowledge** of the **many gifts** I have received, that filled with **gratitude** for all, I may in all things **love and serve God and others** (the Divine majesty).
>
> In calling me to live **my special qualities and characteristics,** God planted in me an **original purpose**—the concrete expression of God's

hopes in me and for me. My life is to **discover** in
myself that **purpose**—what my concrete, authentic self adds up to—and to **live it out** in my life.

We'll go deeper into a discussion of purpose in chapter 5. On
to the fourth pillar.

Generativity is the fourth pillar. Generativity, in this context, is the
passing down to those in the generations coming behind us the wisdom
and knowledge we have acquired in life. It addresses the question of
what difference our lives will make in this world. It is about the impact
we have on our families, friends, our work, and our communities.

Generativity is about a life of meaningful connections to and
caring for future generations—offering whatever we know they might
find useful—and, even more, staying in contact with young people
and listening to them. It is born of a deep desire to change the world,
to transmit values, and to leave the world better than we found it.

In his book *How to Live Forever—The Enduring Power of
Connecting the Generations*, Marc Friedman makes the case for intergenerational interaction and interdependence—an alliance of talents
that brings joy, empowerment, and abundance to both youth and old
age. He poses this big question: How can we tap the vast and largely
underutilized talent of the older population of men and women in
helping to alleviate the unmet needs of young people and to support
the next generation in ways that fit contemporary realities?

Proximity and close relationships, caring, and connections are
key to realizing this promise and answering Friedman's big question.

Several examples of intergenerational programs come to mind,
including Experience Corps, Encore.org, Big Brothers Big Sisters, and
an intergenerational housing project sponsored by the Mercy Sisters.

The Experience Corps, founded by the AARP Foundation, is a
proven program made up of volunteers who are dedicated to helping children become great readers before completing third grade.
Working collaboratively with teachers, volunteers can change the
course of a child's life by sharing their wisdom and experience.

The Encore Network is a coalition of leaders who champion the civic, social, and economic contributions of people fifty-plus by creating community, stimulating learning, and inspiring action to transform the encore stage of life.

Big Brothers Big Sisters operates under the belief that inherent in every child is incredible potential. Big Brothers Big Sisters makes meaningful, monitored matches between adult volunteers ("Bigs") and children ("Littles") ages five through young adulthood in communities across the country.

The Mercy Sisters sponsor Mercy Housing, a leading affordable housing organization, working to eliminate homelessness and housing insecurity for families, seniors, individuals, and people with disabilities who lack the economic resources to access quality and safe housing opportunities. They work with residents and partners to establish engaged, strong, and inclusive communities.

These intergenerational examples contrast with what some have termed "age apartheid," as may be experienced in places like Sun City, Arizona, and other communities that tend to isolate the older generations from the younger ones.

Generativity involves the desire and act of giving ourselves, in some small or large way, to the needs of the rest of the world. This may be the single most important function of old age. *It is about legacy.*

> What we are inclined to forget is that each of us leaves a legacy, whether we mean to, whether we want to or not. Our legacies are the quality of the lives we leave behind…What are we leaving behind? That is the question that marks the timbre (tone) of a lifetime. (Chittister, *The Gift of Years*)

> One of the greatest legacies a person can leave is a moral ecology—a system of belief and behavior that lives on after they die… Moral ecologies subtly guide how you define your ultimate purpose. (David Brooks, *The Second Mountain: The Quest for a Moral Life*, 4)

One of the best ways for us to promote generativity and capture the legacy we would like to leave behind is to write what is called an "ethical will." This is different from the will you have probably already written as part of your estate planning, which sets forth your wishes regarding the distribution of your assets and belongings after you die. The ethical will is a document that passes ethical values from one generation to the next and demonstrates the impact these values can have. The goal of writing an ethical will is to link a person to both their family and cultural history, clarify their ethical and spiritual values, and communicate the difference they hope their life will have made for the generations coming behind them. Writing an ethical will help clarify our identity and focus our life's purpose.

An ethical will captures what we want to leave behind, especially our attitude toward the world and the value system that marks everything we do. Our legacy is far more than our possessions and our fiscal worth. Our legacy does not end the day we die; hopefully, it lives on in those who come behind us.

For years, I have been encouraging others to write an ethical will. Did I write one for myself? No. That changed when I turned eighty. It was time for me to practice what I had been preaching.

I composed the ethical will and decided that the time to share it with my wife, Kathy, our four daughters and sons-in-law, and our twelve grandchildren would be at the family celebration of my eightieth birthday. What a blessing it was for me to read this to them as we were gathered in a circle in our backyard. I had no idea the impact of this on me and on all of them as I shared my deepest hopes and dreams for what I wanted my life to mean for them and for all those whose lives I may have touched over the span of my eighty years. But even more was the impact it made on my family and the way it opened us to communication on a much deeper level.

But the biggest surprise was when the grandkids said, "Poppo, we have letters we want to share with you." Each of them had composed their own letters, telling me what I meant to them! I was left speechless as they told me how much and why they loved me. So much of what they were saying to me about what I meant to them mirrored my hopes and dreams for what, in my legacy letter, I had said

I wanted my life to mean to them. It was an overwhelming moment that I will treasure forever. I had the feeling that if I died right there and then, my life's meaning and purpose would be complete.

For help in getting started on writing your own ethical will, the following resources may be helpful:

- *Step by Step Directions: How to Write an Ethical Will in Six Easy Steps* by Jamie Ruben
- *Ethical Wills: The Gift of a Heart* by Robert G. Alexander
- *Ethical Wills—What They Are and How to Write One* by Kari Berit
- *Ethical Wills and How to Prepare Them* by Rabbi Jack Riemer and Dr. Nathaniel Stampfe

I close this chapter with another of my favorite poems. This one is by Dawna Markova:

I Will Not Die an Unlived Life

I will not die an unlived life
I will not live in fear
of falling or catching fire.
I choose to inhabit my days,
to allow my living to open me,
to make me less afraid,
more accessible,
to loosen my heart
until it becomes a wing,
a torch, a promise.
I choose to risk my significance;
to live so that which came to me as seed
goes to the next as blossom
and that which came to me as blossom,
goes on as fruit.

CHAPTER 5

EXPLORING IDENTITY, MEANING, AND PURPOSE

So much of the process of retiring and growing older involves coming to a new and deeper appreciation of who we are, our self-identity—the "who am I" question—in terms of my true self, my authentic self, not the *persona* I have fashioned for public consumption over the years with its emphasis on employment and activities.

Earlier in our lives, our jobs and our families provided us with plenty of meaning, fulfillment, and a strong sense of identity. Now that those years are behind us (or will be at some point soon), several questions surface: Who am I at this stage of life? Who am I now that I am no longer doing what I used to do? Who am I when I am not defined by my role for others? How has my sense of purpose changed? What do I want the remainder of my life to be and to mean?

Joan Chittister puts it this way:

> This is the time of **coming home to the self**. I find myself stripped of all the accessories of life now. I am face-to-face with *my* self. And the fear is that there isn't one. I have spent my life trying to be someone important, and now there is nothing left but me. I no longer run anything, I have no job responsibilities, I'm not becoming anything. I'm just me now. And what is that? (Chittister, *The Gift of Years*)

This reality is beautifully captured in a favorite poem of mine by May Sarton, "Now I Become Myself." Read it slowly and let her words and meaning become your own.

> Now I become myself. It's taken
> Time, many years and places;
> I have been dissolved and shaken,
> Worn other people's faces,
>
> Run madly, as if Time were there,
> Terribly old, crying a warning,
> "Hurry, you will be dead before—"
> (What? Before you reach the morning?
> Or the end of the poem is clear?
> Or love safe in the walled city?)
>
> Now to stand still, to be here,
> Feel my own weight and density!
> The black shadow on the paper
> Is my hand; the shadow of a word
> As thought shapes the shaper
> Falls heavy on the page, is heard.
>
> All fuses now, falls into place
> From wish to action, word to silence,
> My work, my love, my time, my face
> Gathered into one intense
> Gesture of growing like a plant.
>
> As slowly as the ripening fruit
> Fertile, detached, and always spent,
> Falls but does not exhaust the root,
> So all the poem is, can give,
> Grows in me to become the song,
> Made so and rooted by love.

Now there is time and Time is young.
O, in this single hour I live
All of myself and do not move.
I, the pursued, who madly ran,
Stand still, stand still, and stop the sun!

Growing older is certainly a time of coming home to the self. As we get older, we often become more and more ourselves… We grow into our individuality. It is a period in life where each of us has the time and freedom to bring forth what is in us and to continue in new ways to use our own giftedness to make a difference. For St. Francis of Assisi, the most important question was this: "What is mine to do?" In other words, how will I choose to put my giftedness into doing something for others?

Leider and Shapiro put it this way in their book *Claiming Your Place at the Fire: Living the Second Half of Your Life on Purpose:*

> Perhaps no challenge is greater for people in the second half of life than to find something meaningful and valuable to do with their gifts… New elders find deep satisfaction in giving their gifts in new ways that serve others rather than just themselves. And they accept this as a critical responsibility of their elderhood.

Wendy Lustbader, in her book *Life Gets Better—The Unexpected Pleasures of Growing Older*, says this:

> Later life is the time when we tend to have room in our lives for generosity.
>
> It gives us reasons to prevail over our personal difficulties and grants us access to vital sources of renewal. We find there is strength in doing what good we can for others, not as an intellectual construct but as a robust way of meeting each day.

Coming to a new understanding and appreciation of who we are and finding something meaningful and valuable to do with our gifts are perhaps the greatest challenges at this stage of life.

David Brooks, in his book *The Second Mountain: The Quest for a Moral Life*, frames the challenge perfectly:

> It is about how to give your life meaning after worldly success has failed to fulfill. Moving from a self-centered, hyper-individualistic way of life, to other centeredness, from acquisition (first mountain) to contribution (second mountain); a more generous and satisfying phase of life characterized by a re-fashioned, re-imagined sense of purpose focused on generosity that transforms them and brings them joy—physical, moral, emotional, spiritual, and transcendent.
>
> To live with joy is to live with wonder, delight, gratitude, and hope!

It is that sense of purpose that gives us our identity. The Trappist monk Thomas Merton makes this point by raising two questions. The first is this:

> If you want to identify me, ask not where I live, or what I like to eat, or how I comb my hair, but ask me *what I think I am living for, in detail.*

It is that sense of life purpose that is so critical. It is in our clear and detailed answer to that question that we define who we are.

His second question is the zinger:

> And ask me *what I think is keeping me from living fully the things I want to live for.*

The point Merton makes is that it is one thing to describe what our life purpose is; it is another thing to live out our life purpose.

There may be some things that are holding us back from the full living of our life purpose. When I have asked groups in my workshops and retreats what those things holding us back might be, the number one answer has been fear.

This fear can be evident in two different ways. It can be a fear of failing. We could define our life's purpose and fall short of what we had envisioned for ourselves. How will I deal with that sense of failure? Or it could be a fear of success. If I succeed, how will that success change my life in unexpected ways?

In any case, if we are afraid, it is important to name our fear. What am I afraid of? And why? Perhaps a better way of phrasing the question is this: What would I be doing and how would I be living if I were not afraid?

Fear can immobilize us, blocking us from moving forward. It grips us and can hold us hostage from attaining our hopes and dreams. Fear is different from caution. Caution, in a positive way, leads us to think first, stop for a moment to assess the situation, and then move forward.

Once we have faced the issue of fear, then we can get back to the important work of living out our life purpose. If we don't, then the consequence is likely to be a deep sense of regret.

There was a study done by a hospice nurse. She asked her patients to name their top regrets about dying. The top responses were "not being true to myself" and "not living the life I was intended to live."

The author Parker Palmer captures the sense of regret this way:

> I can't think of a sadder way to die than
> with the knowledge that I never showed up in
> this world as who I really am.

And Daniel Leary, in an article entitled "Home Before Dark," said this:

> Nothing is so sad as regretting, on our
> deathbed, our unlived lives, our untold stories,
> our unsung songs.

In contrast, St. Francis of Assisi said this on his deathbed: "I have done what I was born to do." He was able to say this because he had answered for himself the two questions he felt were central to his calling: "To what do I want to give myself?" and "What is mine to do?" Would that we all could express that same sense of completion and fulfillment when we are dying.

St. Ignatius had this to say about *purpose*:

> *In calling me to live **my special qualities and characteristics,** God planted in me an **original purpose**—the concrete expression of God's hopes in me and for me.*
>
> *My life is to **discover** in myself that **purpose**—what my concrete, authentic self adds up to—and to **live it out** in my life.*

If I grow to be the person God was hoping I would become, I manifest God's power at work—God's glory. In the words of St. Irenaeus, "The glory of God is a human person fully alive."

Leider and Shapiro have this to say about our life purpose:

> Ultimately, it is not so much a matter of *finding* a purpose that gives us such true joy as it is a matter of *recognizing* what our purpose already is and *claiming* it. And when we are able to claim it—and live it—we will have taken what is perhaps the most important step of all to growing whole, not old, in the second half of life. (Leider/Shapiro, *Claiming Your Place at the Fire: Living the Second Half of Your Life on Purpose*)

> The true expression of our life's purpose is as vital to our ending as to our beginning. Heeding our call keeps us journeying on purpose—and thus growing and evolving to the very end of our lives. We may retire from our jobs but

there is no relaxing from our individual callings. **Callings never end when careers do.** Our vocational story unfolds from cradle to grave. (Leider/Shapiro)

The notion of reclaiming our purpose and meaning is not new—the essential questions facing us have not really changed over time. What is new, at least to some extent, is the degree of freedom [time and hopefully financial] and longevity we now have in the second half of life to develop our own answers free of previous responsibilities, pressures, constraints. (Leider/Shapiro)

As we develop these answers, we should be conscious of the Spirit working within us, leading us to listen to the whisperings of our hearts, and increasing our awareness of our own deepest desires and sense of purpose.

So what is meant by the word *purpose*? Purpose is about what concerns us the most, what we care about, and what gets us moving. Purpose gives us something to live for. It determines how we spend our precious time and resources. Purpose energizes and motivates. Purpose is the anchor that secures our lives. When our sense of purpose dies, so does vitality.

Our personal sense of purpose is grounded in our desire to meet a particular need—in our family, in our community, and in our world.

It is in identifying needs and finding a way to fill them that we find something to live for in life. Without something to live for, life is not worth living, and only by living with the love of God and the concerns and needs of others on our hearts can we live in a way that sustains us day after day.

St. Teresa of Avila put it this way:

As we explore the deep calling of our lives, may we be filled with hope for the peace, justice, and ecological wholeness of all peoples on earth. May we struggle with the way our sense of our personal life calling relates to the needs of the world.

Thomas Merton said this about his own struggle with his sense of purpose:

> I am obscurely convinced that there is a need in the world for something I can provide… and there is a need for me to provide it. Someone else can do it, but God is asking me to do it.

In short, reimagining our vocational journey and sense of purpose as we age involves both a recognition of our gifts and an exploration of the world's needs, trying to see where our gifts and the needs of the world might intersect. Parker Palmer puts it this way:

> When I die, I won't be asking about the bottom line. I'll be asking if I was faithful to my gifts, to the needs I saw around me, and to the ways I engaged those needs with my gifts.

So, to address this challenge of clarifying and reimagining what we want the purpose of our lives to be, it may be helpful to raise some questions, the answers to which will help you come to greater clarity about the sense of purpose that will guide your years yet to be lived. Take the time to reflect on them:

- What are you living for, hoping for?
- What excites you, brings you joy, and makes you come alive? What are you passionate about? What gets your adrenaline going?
- What personal pains and sufferings are on your heart? What pains and sufferings on behalf of the world are particularly on your heart?

- How do you want to make a difference? If you feel any type of call (tug, pull, dream, inclination, or desire) to do *something* to meet the needs and concerns of the world around you, regardless of your background and experience, how would you describe it?
- How can you respond with creativity and generosity to address, in your own unique way, these needs/concerns?
- What footprint do you hope to leave on this earth as your legacy?

Carve out some time now to summarize your thoughts and feelings using the following reflective exercise:

REFLECTIVE EXERCISE NUMBER 6:
THE MEANING AND PURPOSE OF YOUR LIFE NOW AND AS YOU LOOK AHEAD TO THE YEARS TO COME

- *As you think about your life now and as you look to the years to come, how would you describe the meaning and purpose of your life going forward?*
- *What are the needs/issues/activities about which you are most excited and to which you are most drawn?*
- *How do your gifts, talents, and desires connect to these needs?*
- *As you look to the years ahead, do you see the meaning and purpose of your life changing? If yes, how and why?*

In addition to the above reflective exercise, there are two other ways of helping to clarify and define the meaning you hope your life will have and the legacy you hope to leave.

The first is one we have already talked about in chapter 4—*writing an ethical will.* Again, different from your last will and testament, which delineates how you would like your tangible personal assets distributed, the ethical will speaks to the values and beliefs you have held fast to in your life and which you have tried to pass on to those with whom you have interacted over your lifetime.

The second is *writing your own obituary.* While some find this on the morbid side, it is a helpful way to capture what you hope will be said about you at the end of your life. Think first of what you would like said about your role in your family—as spouse, parent, grandparent, aunt, or uncle. Write about the love you have shared, the lessons you have tried to teach, and the values you hope will be passed on to the generations coming behind you. You might even allude to any failures or unfulfilled hopes and what you have learned from them. Your obituary should also say something about how you have defined your mission in life, the major roles you have had in your career, and the impact you hope your work has had and on whom.

So, to continue your reflection on the meaning and purpose of your life, the next step is to take a closer look at your deepest desires and longings for the years ahead. This is important because it is often in clarifying, defining, and pursuing your deepest desires that you find your sense of purpose. How we uncover our deepest desires will be covered in the next chapter.

I recognize that all the reflective Exercises I am recommending take time and effort. Believe me, it is worth the time and effort! Be patient with yourselves and take to heart the words of Pierre Teilhard de Chardin (1881–1955), a French Jesuit, paleontologist, biologist, and philosopher:

Trust in the Slow Work of God

Above all, trust in the slow work of God.
We are quite naturally impatient in everything
to reach the end without delay.
We should like to skip the intermediate stages.
We are impatient of being on the way to
something unknown, something new.
Yet it is the law of all progress that is made by
passing through some stages of instability and
that may take a very long time.

And so I think it is with you. Your ideas mature
gradually. Let them grow. Let them shape themselves
without undue haste. Do not try to force them on as though
you could be today what time that is to say, grace—and
circumstances acting on your own good will will make you
tomorrow.
Only God could say what this new Spirit gradually
forming in you will be. Give our Lord the benefit of
believing that his hand is leading you, and accept
the anxiety of feeling yourself in suspense and incomplete.

Above all, trust in the slow work of God, our loving
vine-dresser. Amen.

CHAPTER 6

UNCOVERING YOUR DEEPEST DESIRES

Central to finding your sense of meaning and purpose is exploring, clarifying, and defining your deepest desires. Yet, as pointed out on the website *Ignatianspiritualiy.com*, the importance of desire in Ignatian spirituality is not discussed enough. This website is sponsored by Loyola Press and is a rich resource for coming to understand the essentials of Ignatian spirituality. Here is a summary of what the website says about the importance of paying attention to our deepest desires.

Saint Ignatius uses this word *desire* throughout *The Spiritual Exercises*. He says that one of the purposes of the exercises is "to find better what one desires." Our desires, like many things, are a way God communicates with our heart, guides us, and calls us. Ultimately, we see that our desires are really the same as God's desires for us. They lead us to the person God wants us to become. When we find out what we really want, we also find out what God wants because God has planted his desires in our hearts. In other words, our truest desires reflect God's desires in us and for us.

The spiritual writer Richard Rohr expressed it simply and beautifully this way: "Would it not make sense that God would plant in us a desire for what God already wants to give us. I am sure of it" (Rohr, *Falling Upward*).

The best way to discover our truest desires is to bring ourselves to prayer and spend time with our questions, our hurts and fears, and our dreams. In prayer and over time, we can allow the Holy Spirit to sift through all of it, until what remains is what we truly long for— our deepest needs and wants.

This is the work of the Spirit—leading us to listen to the whisperings of our hearts and increasing our awareness of our own deepest desires and the sense of purpose that emerges from them.

I turn again to the words of David Brooks regarding the potency of God's love and grace relative to our desires:

> A believer approaches God with a humble reverence and comes, through study and prayer and the spiritual disciplines, to get a feel for the grain of God's love. She gradually learns to live along the grain of God's love and not against the grain… Faith and grace are not about losing agency. They are about strengthening and empowering agency while transforming it. When grace floods in, it gives us better things to desire and more power to desire them. When people talk about dying to self, they are really talking about dying to old desires and coming alive to a new and better set of desires. (David Brooks, *Second Mountain*, 255)

So, as a next step in the process of discerning what's next in your life, it is important to explore and articulate your deepest desires for the years ahead.

The quest to uncover your deepest desires is a journey that resonates with all of us. It is an exploration of our innermost passions and aspirations, a pursuit that holds the key to unlocking our fullest potential and defining our life's purpose. Here is a reflective exercise to assist you in this process.

REFLECTIVE EXERCISE NUMBER 7
EXPLORING YOUR DEEPEST DESIRES

The first step toward exploring your deepest desires is to pause and reflect. Take some moments of solitude to detach yourself from the noise and distractions of the outside world. Use this exercise to delve into the depths of your heart and mind, exploring the passions that stir your soul. Listen to your inner voice and pay attention to the whispers of your heart.

As you think about your life now and as you look to the years to come, develop a clear statement that captures your deepest desires and longings for

- *deepening or healing your relationship with your family (spouse, children, and grandchildren) and your closest friends;*
- *deepening your relationship with God and enlivening your spiritual life;*
- *deepening and pursuing your most enjoyable leisure pursuits (e.g., travel, reading, favorite hobbies, etc.);*
- *deepening your commitment to your community and the broader world and your desires to give back by using your gifts and talents to meet a need about which you are passionate.*

In responding to this last bullet point, the assumption is that you have a good understanding and appreciation for your giftedness and that you desire to use those gifts in service of a need that stirs your heart. As you develop your response, it will be helpful to go back to chapter 3 and your efforts to clearly identify your gifts and talents.

You can use the template below to organize your thoughts and come to greater clarity about your deepest desires. Write them out in a way that describes them with some specificity and that captures their importance for you on a personal level. If you keep a journal, use your journal to record your thoughts and reflections.

- My deepest desires for healing or deepening my relationship with family and friends include the following:
- My deepest desires for deepening my relationship with God and enlivening my spiritual life include the following:
- My deepest desires for pursuing my most rewarding leisure pursuits include the following:
- My deepest desires for using my gifts and talents through an action project to give back by meeting a need about which I am passionate

Include the following elements in the description of your action project:

o   I desire a project/service/ministry where my *top skills and abilities* in... (Name the skills and abilities that are both among your strongest and the ones you most enjoy using.)

o   and my character strengths/personal qualities of ... (If you need some help with this one, try taking the "Character Strengths Inventory" at *authentic happiness.com.*)

o   can be combined with my *specialized knowledge and experience* in... (Name the areas of expertise that you would most like to continue to share in making a difference in the world.)

o   in order to *serve the purpose or meet the need* in my community, in society, or in my church, synagogue, or mosque for... (Respond in terms of the top specific role, societal need, issue, passion, or concern to which you are most drawn.)

o   I would like to pursue this work/service/ministry in the *organizational culture/setting* of a... (What are the organizational values and characteristics that would be most conducive to the effectiveness of your service?)

o   Preferably, I would like my work/service/ministry to be centered in *the geographical area* of... (Assuming you are not looking for a geographical change, this would be in the area where you are currently living; or maybe you are looking to make a geographical move to a new area; or maybe you are even considering a temporary relocation to an area in need of your service.).

In pursuing your deepest desires, be sure to ensure *balance in your life*. Allow yourself the time and energy for all three dimensions—family and friends, spiritual practices, and a work/service commitment. but do not overlook carving out time for the fun and the frivolous, including leisure pursuits such as recreational, cultural, and health-related activities. You may want to list or describe these other pursuits and activities that you hope to make a part of your life and how you intend to achieve the balance we all desire.

Each of the elements of this template is intended to provide additional clarity and focus for your discernment. And the greater the clarity and the sharper the focus, the easier it will be to move on to the next challenge of taking the *action steps* necessary to move from desires to intentions and turn your desires into reality.

Remember, the journey toward discovering your deepest desires and finding your calling is not a linear path. It is a continuous process of growth and self-reflection. Be patient and kind to yourself along the way, for self-discovery takes time. Embrace the twists and turns and the highs and lows, knowing that each step brings you closer to your authentic sense of purpose and a life of fulfillment and meaning (adapted from *Amnesty International* website).

When your statement has been drafted, you may want to share it with family members and a few close friends. Listen to their reactions and answer any questions they may raise. Oftentimes, those who know us best can identify our gifts and talents better than we ourselves. This may be because we don't see anything special about the gifts and talents that may come easiest to us. This sharing with others will help you gain additional clarity and specificity around your deepest desires.

We close this chapter with another of my favorite poems. This one again is from the Irish poet John O'Donohue:

Blessing for Retirement

This is where your life has arrived,
After all the years of effort and toil;
Look back with graciousness and thanks
On all your great and quiet achievements

You stand on the shore of new invitation
To open your life to what is left undone;
Let your heart enjoy a different rhythm
When drawn to the wonder of other horizons.

Have the courage for a new approach to time;
Allow it to slow until you find freedom
To draw alongside the mystery you hold
And befriend your own beauty of soul.

Now is the time to enjoy your heart's desire,
To live the dreams you've waited for,
To awaken the depths beyond your work
And enter into your infinite source.

CHAPTER 7

MOVING FROM YOUR DESIRES AND INTENTIONS TO ACTION

You have spent significant time reflecting on your deepest desires for what is next in your life in three areas: your relationships with family and friends, your relationship with God, and using your gifts and talents to give back to your community, helping meet a need about which you are passionate. Now you are ready to move on to the implementation stage of the process. How do you move from desires to action in a way that will make your desires a reality? In other words, how do you make the future you most desire happen?

This is a topic very well covered in a book by Ron Pevny called *Conscious Living, Conscious Aging*. It is one of the books on my recommended reading list. I have drawn on it for this chapter.

One of the signs of clarity around our discernment of the purpose and meaning of our lives going forward is the *resolve to act*—to move beyond our feelings of desire and longing to intentionality and execution. In short, this is about making real our deepest desires.

So the next step in your discernment process is committing to some actions that will help you achieve your desires for what is next in your life. Begin by reflecting on the steps you are ready to take to help make your deepest desires a reality in your life. As always, it is good to commit your thoughts and intentions in writing. As you do this, use empowering language and set your timeline for achieving each of them. It is not empowering to write. "I hope that…" or "I'd like to…" It is empowering to declare, "Within the next year, I will have…" or "I intend to…"

These intentions should not be mere fantasies but goals that you are committed to achieving within the timeline you set. It is important that you bring the immense power of intention to all aspects of your life as you age. It is important, when approaching your future with such intentionality, that you do your best to have your intentions be more than just inspired words. Envision each of them being accomplished and feel what you imagine you will feel like when they become realities in your life.

One piece of advice: It can be tempting to dream up action plans so big that they become overwhelming and ambiguous. Don't let this happen to you! With every action step you create, be sure to discern the first steps you will take—what will they be? And when will you take these steps?

There are a number of action steps that will help advance your deepest desires. bring clarity to your intentions, and lead you down the path of implementation. Let me touch on some very important ones.

Information gathering is your way of becoming familiar with and conversant around the need you have identified as the one about which you have the passion and desire to make a difference.

The traditional tools of research are ones you are likely already familiar with. These would include internet searches, articles, and books that speak about your area of interest or concern. This should be your starting point so that you have some depth of understanding about the need you hope to help address and about what others are already doing to meet that need.

Once you have this deeper understanding, you will be ready to move on to the next step in your research—*informational interviewing and networking*. This next step serves multiple purposes. It further deepens your understanding of the need you are researching, and it begins to build a network of contacts who will not only help further your understanding but also become your allies in searching for and obtaining the kind of opportunity you are seeking.

Those of you who are familiar with the networking process are likely aware of the usefulness of *LinkedIn* as a tool. LinkedIn can help you reestablish old connections and identify new connections with people who are specifically related to your area(s) of interest.

As important and useful as this tool is, it is no substitute for the people closest to us as part of our network—our family, our friends, and our former work colleagues. Ask yourself, "Who among them do I think would be most helpful to my quest—people whom I can enlist as allies? And how and when do I best communicate with them about what I want to do next in my life?"

A word of advice about networking: Be careful not to make too many assumptions about who (or who not) would be most helpful in your quest to both gather information and enlist allies. You may think you know a person well enough to know whether speaking with them about your interests and plans would be beneficial. However, you can never fully know how helpful any given person might be to you. Sometimes it is people we least expect who turn out to be the most helpful.

Based on the information you have gathered through research and networking, you will find it helpful to expand or refine your description of what you want to do next in your life and the personal assets you bring to the enterprise.

Begin by *developing a narrative description of the need you would like to help address* and the nature of the service or contribution you hope to make in meeting that need.

Another next step in the implementation process is developing a personal résumé. While typically associated with job hunting, composing a résumé can be very helpful in clarifying and summarizing your qualifications and, consequently, the contribution you can make in addressing the need you hope to help meet. The résumé will be especially helpful if what's next for you is volunteering or working for an organization. It has the added benefits of organizing your thoughts and building your case for the contribution you can make to an organization while, at the same time, building your self-confidence.

The steps in developing a résumé include the following:

- setting the position goal or objective (drawn from your narrative statement), including the skills, abilities, and personal qualities you have that are most important to success in that role;
- developing a paragraph describing your experiences that most clearly demonstrates each skill, ability, or personal quality you wish to highlight. This brief paragraph should include a succinct description of what you accomplished, how you did it, and qualifying and quantifying the results when possible.
- structuring the sections of the résumé. Key sections include your position goal or objective; a summary of key accomplishments organized by skill areas, work history, education, and personal, depending on the format you choose. A basic rule of thumb is to put first in your résumé those qualifications that are most relevant to the kind of volunteer opportunity or position you are pursuing.

There are three different formats you can use in developing your résumé: chronological, functional, or hybrid.

The *chronological format* organizes your information according to the dates you were engaged with the organizations for whom you have worked, usually starting with the most recent and working your way backward over your work history. Each entry should note the dates of your employment, the name of your employer, and a brief description of your duties and responsibilities. It is also important to include any special accomplishments or achievements you had while in this position.

The *functional format* organizes your materials according to your key skills, abilities, and personal qualities. You name the skill area and then describe the work experiences you have had where you demonstrated that skill, again noting any special accomplishments or achievements you had where this skill was key.

The *hybrid format* is just what you would think—a combination of both the chronological and functional formats. This gives you some flexibility in how you present your information and allows you to lead with those experiences or skills that most clearly show the strength of your qualifications for the opportunity you are seeking.

Remember, this résumé is not for a job search but for a volunteer opportunity. It can serve multiple purposes. First, it can be used to help secure an informational interview with the person inside the organization who is responsible for coordinating volunteers. Second, it helps you to make your case for why you would add value to the organization where you want to volunteer. Even if you are not using your résumé in connection with a volunteer activity, it provides a useful summary of the gifts and talents you have to offer. Third, it provides a guide for the person you are interviewing to discuss your qualifications with you. And, lastly, it gives the organization something to hold on to as a record and reminder of your conversation.

In addition to preparing your résumé, it is important to think ahead to the informational interview itself and how you might structure it. First, be clear about the purpose of the interview. You are seeking more information about the organization and the volunteer opportunities it offers. Once you have covered these points and are clear about the needs of the organization, it is time to talk about your own personal interest in volunteering and the experience, gifts, and talents you would bring to the organization to help them meet their needs. Finally, be sure you have a good understanding of what the organization expects from its volunteers—the types of work the volunteers do, the expectations of the organization in terms of a time commitment, etc. Be sure to get all your questions answered before you end the interview.

And one more thing: never leave an informational interview without asking for any recommendations this person might have about other people they suggest you also speak with about your interests. This is the way your network can be easily and quickly expanded.

Once you have finished this conversation, you should spend some time evaluating what you have learned. Here are some questions that might be helpful to your evaluation:

- Do I understand and support the purpose of this organization?
- Do I resonate with the people with whom and for whom I would be working?
- Do I have a clear understanding of what the volunteer opportunities involve—the type of work I would be doing. the time commitment expected, etc.?
- Is this an environment where I can be happy and productive?
- Do my interests, skills, and experience match the volunteer opportunities offered by this organization?

With all this as background, it is time to put together a sketch of what your *action plan* will be. One of the signs of clarity around our discernment of the purpose and meaning of our lives going forward is the emerging *resolve to act*—to move beyond our feelings of desire and longing to a commitment to intentionality and execution. The action plan involves committing to some action steps that will help you achieve your desires for what is next in your life.

Please take time to complete the next reflective exercise as a way of more clearly defining the next action steps you need to take.

REFLECTIVE EXERCISE NUMBER 8
MOVING FROM DESIRES TO INTENTIONS: A
TEMPLATE FOR AN ACTION/PROJECT PLAN

You recently developed a statement of your deepest desires for each of the four major life dimensions that provide meaning and purpose to our lives: relationships with family and friends, relationship with God and a deeper spiritual life, pursuit of enjoyable leisure activities, and a work/service/ministry where you can use your gifts and talents to meet a need. Now we recommend you draft in writing the action steps you need to take in each of these areas.

These intentions or action steps should not be mere fantasies but goals that you are committed to achieving within the timeline you set. It is important, when approaching your future with such intentionality, that you do your best to have your intentions be more than just inspired words. Envision each of them being accomplished and imagine what you will feel like when they become realities in your life.

It can be tempting to dream up action plans so big that they become overwhelming and ambiguous. Don't let this happen to you! With each action that you create and commit to, be sure to also answer these two questions: What will the first steps be in taking this action? And when will these steps be taken? A timeline is essential to following through on your action plan.

Developing your action plan is an important next step. Don't be overwhelmed by the task. Know that the most important thing is to determine the next steps you need to take to make them real in your life.

My Action Plan—The Next Steps I Need to Take

Next Steps   Sources of Help   Date of Completion

CHAPTER 8

THE SPIRITUAL DIMENSION OF DISCERNING YOUR FUTURE

The process of reflecting on the important steps of discernment can be approached in a strictly rational manner, weighing the pros and cons of the different options that may be possible and making choices based solely on our own individual desires. However, for those who come from a strong faith tradition, discernment is much more than that. It considers not just your personal wishes and desires but also what may be God's desires for you and how God may be calling you to follow a certain path or head in a certain direction. In other words, as pointed out in chapter 3, there is a spiritual dimension to discernment. So what does this entail, and what is a "spiritual life"?

Too often, the spiritual life is associated only with prayer or contemplation, but the spiritual life also includes action, service, and activities. This is manifested beautifully in the account of Jesus washing the feet of the apostles. As Pope Francis says, "We are all called to be foot washers!" We are spiritual, not just when we are in private prayer mode but when we are recognizing God's presence in all aspects of our lives and when we are using our gifts to love and serve those with whom we are in contact in our daily lives.

This is the *call to holiness* that Pope Francis speaks so eloquently and clearly about in his letter, "On the Call to Holiness":

> Everything can be accepted and integrated
> into our life in this world and become a part of

our path to holiness. We are called to be **contemplatives even in the midst of action,** and to grow in holiness by responsibly and generously carrying out our proper mission.

He goes on to say:

> We need to see the entirety of our life as a mission. Try to do so by listening to God in prayer and recognizing the signs that he gives you. Always ask the Spirit what Jesus expects from you at every moment of your life and in every decision you must make, so as to discern its place in the mission you have received. Allow the Spirit to forge in you the personal mystery that can reflect Jesus Christ in today's world.

Pope Francis, as a Jesuit, is a proponent of the spirituality of St. Ignatius. One of the tenets of Ignatian spirituality is *finding God in all things*—prayer, service, and the activities of our daily routine. It is possible to encounter Christ in both our active service and our prayer and contemplation.

Meister Eckhart, a Dominican theologian and writer (1260–1327), put it beautifully and succinctly:

> What we plant in the soil of contemplation,
> we shall reap in the harvest of action.

The reverse is also true: what we sow in the soil of action, we shall reap in the harvest of contemplation. There is a beautiful reciprocity between contemplation and action!

We may often think that our lives and our activities in the world take us away from God. Far from that; our active life in the world is meant to be the very place of our encounter with Christ. This is especially true when we are responding positively to the needs of others.

There is no more important passage from the Gospels that makes this very point than Matthew 25:31–40:

> When the Son of Man comes in his glory, and all the angels with him, he will sit on his glorious throne. All the nations will be gathered before him, and he will separate the people one from another as a shepherd separates the sheep from the goats. He will put the sheep on his right and the goats on his left.
>
> Then the King will say to those on his right, "Come, you who are blessed by my Father; take your inheritance, the kingdom prepared for you since the creation of the world. For I was hungry and you gave me something to eat, I was thirsty and you gave me something to drink, I was a stranger and you invited me in, I needed clothes and you clothed me, I was sick and you looked after me, I was in prison and you came to visit me."
>
> Then the righteous will answer him, "Lord, when did we see you hungry and feed you, or thirsty and give you something to drink? When did we see you a stranger and invite you in, or needing clothes and clothe you? When did we see you sick or in prison and go to visit you?"
>
> The King will reply, "Truly I tell you, whatever you did for one of the least of these brothers and sisters of mine, you did for me."

Pope Francis has some beautiful words to explain how God's love for us should be manifested in our love for our neighbor:

> *For if we have received the love that restores meaning to our lives, how can we fail to share that love with others?*

> *Our invitation to receive God's love and to love him in return, brings forth in our lives and actions a primary and fundamental response—to desire, seek, and protect the good of others.*
>
> *An authentic faith—which is never comfortable or completely personal—always involves a deep desire to change the world, to transmit values, to leave this earth somehow better than we found it.*

The goal of the spiritual life then is to develop a consciousness of God being ever present in our lives, guiding, supporting, and challenging us in all that we do in our daily lives—family, work, recreation, social life, etc.—and to make prayer fully natural, like breathing.

As noted earlier in chapter 1, one of the essential elements of a good retirement and conscious, purposeful aging is having a consistent spiritual or prayer practice in our lives. While some would say this is a requirement, I like to see it more as an invitation or a response to God's love for us. God wants to engage us in a personal relationship—a conversation. Whether or not we hear that call or pay attention, God continues to invite us.

Nurturing the relationship requires making time to talk and listen to God, sharing our joys, hopes, and concerns. Relationships require a two-way dialogue. This dialogue makes our faith interactive and relational.

The basis of prayer is our belief that God dwells inside us (at the very core of our being) and all around us. Spiritual writers call this the *divine indwelling*. Pope Francis tells us that this presence/indwelling calls us to a "personal encounter with Christ or at least an openness to letting him encounter us" ("Joy of the Gospel"). We need to "tune in" to God's presence and deepen our desire for a deeper consciousness of God's presence in our lives.

It is helpful—I would even say essential—to make a conscious effort to enter into this awareness and have this conversation. Here are *some tips to ground your prayer life* as contemplatives in action: stopping, reflecting, sharing, and acting.

In the Gospels, we hear about Jesus and his disciples retreating every so often to pray. Their ministry didn't seem to allow much time for it, but if they hadn't stopped every so often, they might have become mindless in their activity. This is the first step in being a contemplative in action: *stopping* and making time for God and appreciating God's gift of love and presence.

When you set your daily schedule, put your prayer time down first, preferably first thing in the morning. Develop the habit of praying at about the same time and same place each day (prayer space). When we schedule work and other things first, there is little or no time left for prayer; we squeeze God in or don't find any time at all. Often, prayer is the first thing that disappears from our schedule. Aim for constancy and consistency.

To begin your prayer, find a place free of distractions. Choose a posture that is comfortable. Take several minutes to simply listen to the sound of your breathing. Find the stillness and quiet.

Stopping gives you a chance to pause and acknowledge what you've been doing, whether in your work or personal life. It not only offers needed rest but also helps you move into the next stage: *reflection.*

Jesus and the apostles spoke to each other about all they did; they prayed, pondered, and examined their feelings and experiences.

> *The apostles gathered around Jesus and reported to him all they had done and taught. (Mark 6:30)*

Reflecting on our daily experiences—especially the major ones—and *sharing them* helps us delve into their deeper meaning. What did you learn from your experiences? What might God be telling you through them? Opportunities for this sharing are many. Faith sharing with your spouse and close friends, prayer groups, Bible study, and spiritual direction come immediately to mind.

Spiritual life is not something separate from real life. It must be connected. It must be relevant; it must result in *action.*

Contemplation allows us to renew our active lives (work, play, family, relationships) so that all we do does not become mindless action but rather is done with the awareness that we are followers of Christ; our actions glorify God. Then the cycle repeats in an infinite loop. Your activity/service leads you again into a time of stopping, resting, reflecting, and then returning to activity with greater zeal and purpose. Being a contemplative in action means that your active life feeds your contemplative life, and your contemplative life informs your active life. That is what contemplatives in action means, and the cycle never ends.

Here is how Pope Francis expressed this connection in "Joy of the Gospel," number 272:

> When we live out a spirituality of drawing nearer to others and seeking their welfare, our hearts are opened wide to the Lord's greatest and most beautiful gifts. Whenever we encounter another person in love, we learn something new about God. Whenever our eyes are opened to acknowledge the other, we grow in the light of faith and knowledge of God. If we want to advance in the spiritual life, then, we must constantly be missionaries.

The desire for a fuller spiritual life seems to grow in us as we get older. Joan Chittister puts it this way:

> Age is the call to spiritual growth because age finally brings us to the point where there is nowhere else to go but inside for comfort, inside for wealth, inside for the things that really count... It's what's inside of us, not what's outside of us that counts. The interior life, the search for the sacred is what calls us now and we finally have the time—and the freedom to furnish our souls in new ways. (Chittister)

While this call to a deeper interior life is a priority, too often, the spiritual life is associated only with prayer or contemplation. But the spiritual life, as I indicated earlier, also includes action, service, and activities.

Recall again the words of Meister Eckhart: *"What we plant in the soil of contemplation, we shall reap in the harvest of action."* And vice versa.

Contemplative practices are new ways of praying. In the words of Michael Fish, a Trappist monk, "Praying is spending time leaving myself open to what God wants to say to me and do for me." It is a matter of trust.

Bishop Kenneth Untener put it this way:

> There's nothing tricky about prayer. It's
> simply tuning in to God's presence—and God
> is always present. Not simply alongside us, but
> within us at the deepest part of who we are.

Our God is *not* distant and *un*involved in our lives. Rather, God is communicating with us all the time…

- in the universe,
- in nature and the wonders of science,
- through people,
- through the events of our daily lives (happy or sad),
- in the Word of Scripture (particularly in the Gospels, which contain the teachings of Jesus).

Our *response* to God's many ways of communicating with us is what we call prayer. Simply put, prayer is opening ourselves to the presence of God and responding as in any conversation between two persons who love each other.

Again listen to these words from Joan Chittister:

> A blessing of these years is that we are now
> beginning to trust in the life-giving God we do

not see, more than we have trusted in the accessories of life which we have seen and we have learned these accessories both come without guarantee and go without warning.

Living well has something to do with the spirituality of wholeheartedness, of seeing life more as a grace than as a penance, as time to be lived with eager expectation of its goodness, not in dread of its challenges. (Chittister)

Our desire for a deeper consciousness of God's unconditional love and abiding presence in our lives can be satisfied by engaging in any number of contemplative prayer practices. Many of you may already have some contemplative prayer practices that you have made a part of your life. Others of you may not. No matter. I think for either group, it might be helpful to review some of the more popular and highly valued prayer practices. Some, like *lectio divina*, or divine reading, have been around for centuries. Others, like centering prayer, are relatively new.

Let me briefly describe for you some of the more popular contemplative prayer practices.

Lectio Divina

Lectio divina (literally, *divine reading*) is a way of becoming immersed in the Scriptures very personally. It consists of reading God's Word in a moment of prayer and allowing it to enlighten and renew us.

The Christian form of *lectio divina* was first introduced by St. Gregory of Nyssa (c. 330–395), and it was also encouraged by St. Benedict of Nursia (c. 480–547), the founder of the Benedictine Order. It is a way of developing a closer relationship with God by reflecting prayerfully on his words. In *lectio divina*, the chosen spiritual text is read four times in total, giving an opportunity to think deeply about it and respond thoughtfully. When we practice *lectio divina*, we can imagine that we are actually involved in the events of Scripture. Here are the steps to follow:

Begin by finding a comfortable posture. Then quiet yourself by concentrating on your breathing. Take a couple of deep breaths. Inhale God's love. Exhale any worries or concerns about the day.

Read thoughtfully several times the short passage from Scripture you have selected, pausing between each reading as follows:

1. *With the first reading, listen.* The first reading is an opportunity to get to know the Scripture passage. Listen carefully for any words or phrases that stand out for you. It is important not to force things but to wait patiently for God to give gentle guidance.

2. *During the second reading, reflect on what touches you.* The second reading of the same passage focuses further on the points you became aware of during the first reading. Often, it is helpful to reread a few verses so you can reflect carefully on where God may have nudged you. Try not to analyze the passage. It's easy to slip into "study mode" and think about interesting points rather than listening to what God might be saying. It helps to ask God to make his focus clear.

3. *After the third reading, respond by praying about your insight.* You may want to record your thoughts. Writing them down can be helpful. We are sometimes prone to forgetting what we've learned, even by the next day! You can respond in prayer too, which gives you another opportunity for a conversation with God.

4. *Rest—spend some time in silence, listening to what God is saying to you.* Just sit quietly and allow God to work. When your mind starts to wander and dart here and there, bring it gently back to stillness again.

It is important to remember that *lectio divina* is not an end in itself or another spiritual practice to tick off our to-do list. It helps us hear specifically and individually from God through Scripture, guided by the Holy Spirit, deepening our relationship with God.

You may wish to close your *lectio* with a prayer:

> *Loving God, we pray that our lives be filled and overflowing with the power of your love so we can make a difference in this world and bring honor to you. As you have first loved us, help us to love you in return. Help us also to share your love with all those we meet. Help us to use our gifts and talents in your service to help build a community where love and truth, peace, and justice prevail. We ask this through Christ, our Lord. Amen.*

For more helpful resources to guide your *lectio divina*, go to: *https://bustedhalo.com/ministry-resources/lectio-divina-beginners-guide.*

Centering prayer

The simple steps of this method are to choose a sacred word as a symbol of your intention to consent to God's presence and action within. Then, settling comfortably, you introduce the sacred word and remain quietly attentive within God's presence. When distracted from your focus by wandering thoughts, you gently return to the sacred word and your openness to God. After a set period of prayer time, you remain thankful for a minute or two.

This method of directing and sustaining active but receptive openness to God can be extremely challenging for overloaded and distracted minds. Repeatedly, a gentle return to God's presence can be needed—without self-judgment. Yet, over time, the meditative experience can become rewarding. It also generates beneficial changes in personality.

I, too, have felt the transformative power of this ancient but new contemplative prayer. This approach to prayer has three appealing advantages for this twenty-first century's cultural moment:

1. Centering prayer is a completely lay and democratic movement with no need for hierarchical church oversight. It has been called "a monastery without walls."
2. Centering prayer is a self-validating practice that experientially changes its practitioners from within over time. Those drowning in babble and trivial distractions find healing in silence.
3. Centering prayer and contemplation is nondoctrinaire and ecumenical. It can be seen as related to Buddhist and other valued forms of meditation and mindfulness.

Father Thomas Keating, a Cistercian monk, is often recognized as the father of centering prayer. He died in 2018 at the age of ninety-five and, according to his nephew, Peter Jones, had been in poor health for a number of years. He turned to centering prayer based on the encouragement issued by St. Paul VI during the Second Vatican Council to rediscover the contemplative tradition.

Centering prayer, according to author Sidney Callahan, is affirmed by recent developments in neuropsychological research. Today's science reveals the power of the brain/mind's attentional systems to generate mental and physical well-being. Nothing can be as productive for human development as learning to discipline and focus attention. Memory, achievement, and even physical health improve (Cf. *America Magazine*, "Centering Prayer: Contemplative Practice for the 21st Century," by Sidney Callahan, December 3, 2014).

Journaling

Keeping a prayer journal is a personal way to record our prayer experiences and reflections on Scripture. It is a private response. There are no rules as to the form it takes. Over time, a journal can provide a personal history of our life journey and the insights received along the way, like a spiritual autobiography.

The examen of consciousness

It is important to distinguish this prayer practice from the more familiar examination of conscience. The examination of conscience was encouraged as a preparation for the Catholic Sacrament of Reconciliation, or confession, as it is often termed. The examen of consciousness provides the opportunity to review our lives day by day as a way of progressing in our Christian life, deepening our relationship with God and with the people in our lives.

There are five simple steps to the examen as outlined by David Fleming on his website, *ignatianspirituality.com:*

1. *Pray for God's help.* Recall that you are in the presence of God. Pray to the Spirit of God for enlightenment, trust, and freedom to receive whatever surfaces in your memory and whatever God wishes to teach you.
2. *Give thanks for the gifts of this day.* Request that the Spirit lead you through a review of your day. As you review your day, ask God to surface the blessings that you have recently experienced.
3. *Pray over the significant interior moments that surface as you replay the day.* As the moments of blessings surface, reflect on how God has worked for you and been present to you during those moments. Relish and rejoice in the moments that went well and all the gifts you have been given this day.
4. *Repent and seek forgiveness.* Repent of any mistakes or failures—things you could have done better. Ask God to surface moments that need completeness, reconciliation, healing, or attention in any way. Notice how you feel about these moments and ask for the freedom to accept the insights into the cause of those feelings and the lessons learned.
5. *Look to tomorrow.* Resolve, in concrete ways, to live well tomorrow. Pray directly and personally to God in the

words and feelings that surface for you. Pray to deepen or share the blessings you have received. And pray for what you need help with—ways to heal or reconcile those memories that need attention. Close by speaking to God from your heart or with a prayer that is familiar to you, such as the Our Father.

Doing a daily examen has a number of benefits:

- It brings God's presence into all the ups and downs of our day.
- It helps unite us even closer to God and reveal God's perspective on our everyday lives.
- It stirs us to praise God for the countless gifts that have popped up in our day and to find God's presence in those gifts.
- It gives us an opportunity to recognize and apologize for our failures and hurts and receive healing from the experience.
- It brings insight into what is really going on beneath the surface of our thoughts, words, and actions—into the very source of our motivations.
- Lastly, it helps us discern how to handle the trickier aspects of our lives, to know what gifts we need from God to do the right thing tomorrow, and to ask for those gifts explicitly.

Liturgy

The word *liturgy* comes from the Greek word *leitourgia*, referred to as any public service or function exercised by and for the people as a whole. Its importance, especially for Catholics, was captured in this one important sentence from the documents of the Second Vatican Council:

> *The liturgy is the summit toward which the activity of the Church is directed; it is also the font from which all her power flows.* (Vatican Council II, *Sacrosanctum Concilium*)

Liturgy is always an action—something we do; it is not simply a text in a book or a play we watch as spectators. We participate in the action of the liturgy by responding, singing, listening, and joining in the gestures.

The liturgy, then, is our participation in Jesus's prayer, in his obedience, and in self-offering to the Father. Through that participation, the liturgy becomes our work—the "work of the Church...a sacred action surpassing all others."

Two key points:

- The liturgy is key to the life of the church, both nourishing the people of God and inspiring them to fulfill the church's mission.
- The church celebrates its common liturgy universally and publicly as we join our local church in solidarity with the universal church, celebrating the same Eucharistic liturgy throughout the world. This brings home to us the beauty and expansiveness of the church.

In addition to the above prayer forms, there are others that hold an important part in the prayer life of many:

- *Attendance at the daily Mass.* While certainly not required, many Catholics choose to attend Mass on a daily basis. This is a practice that is both praiseworthy and beneficial by drawing on the Eucharist as an invaluable aid, both intellectually and spiritually, in understanding and living the Christian life.
- *The Liturgy of the Hours.* This is an official prayer of the church and the highest form of liturgical prayer after the Mass. It is an ancient, structured way of praying Scripture throughout the day, with a special focus on the Psalms. It continues a practice of the early church of praying at specified times during the day. For guidance on this form of prayer, I recommend Daria Sockey's book, *The Everyday Catholic's Guide to the Liturgy of the Hours.*

- *The Rosary:* The Rosary is a Scripture-based prayer that leads us to Jesus through Mary. It begins with the *Apostles' Creed*, which summarizes the great mysteries of the Catholic faith and centers on the events of Christ's life. There are four sets of Mysteries: Joyful, Sorrowful, Glorious, and—added by Saint John Paul II in 2002—the Luminous. Each decade of the Rosary begins with *Our Father*, which introduces each mystery. It is followed by the recitation of ten *Hail Marys*. As a prayer form, the Rosary is often prayed with these intentions in mind: to help people grow in their faith, convert sinners, and bring about world peace.

- *Contemplative walking* (savoring nature). Contemplative walking does not necessarily mean walking slowly, although at its heart, it is not a rushed activity. When we walk contemplatively, we give ourselves over to the experience, walking with an intentional and reverential heart.

The Center for Action and Contemplation offers the following guidance: As you begin a contemplative walk, allow a few moments simply to breathe and connect to your heart. Set an intention for this time to be as present as you can to what is happening, both within and without. Begin walking, but see if you can release any expectations or destinations. As you walk, imagine that with each step, your feet are both blessing the ground and being blessed by it. Let your breath be long and slow. Bring your awareness to the beauty of the earth all around you.

Notice what draws your attention. Listen to the sounds of life around you. Pause regularly, simply to receive this gift. Breathe it in. Let it have some space in your heart. Then continue on until something else causes you to stop.

This is the whole of the practice: simply moving, listening, and pausing. We practice presence so that we might cultivate our ability to really hear the voice of God speaking to us in the beauty that surrounds us.

For many of us, prayer may not come naturally. Given that this is the case, the church, over the centuries, has developed different forms of prayer. You can see from the above descriptions that there are a variety of forms of prayer that are part of the church's tradition. As you begin to establish a consistent prayer practice in your own life, you may want to experiment with some of these prayer forms to see what works best for the deepening of your own personal relationship with God.

It is also helpful to know that in getting started with a consistent, daily practice of contemplative prayer, people often find it beneficial to use different resources that assist us in our prayer. There are many excellent resources available, both in print and online. Here are some I would recommend:

- *Sacred Space* (available as an online resource as well as an app for tablets and phones) http://www.sacredspace.ie/
- *Give Us This Day*, Liturgical Press, www.giveusthisday.org
- *Living Faith; Daily Catholic Devotions* at www.LivingFaith.com
- Daily "3-Minute Retreats" at http://www.loyolapress.com/3-minute-retreats-daily-online-prayer
- Daily reflections from the Center for Action and Contemplation; Fr. Richard Rohr at https://cac.org/
- *Reimagining the Examen* at http://www.ignatianspirituality.com/23542/reimagining-examen-app

If you find any of these intriguing, I encourage you to give them a try and decide what best suits your personality and your needs for having a deeper sense of God's presence and acting in your life.

Remember, the goal of the spiritual life is to develop a deeper consciousness of God's unconditional love for us and of God being ever present in our lives, guiding, supporting, and challenging us in all that we do in our daily lives—family, work, recreation, social life, etc.—and to make prayer fully natural, like breathing.

One final recommendation: as you strive to deepen your spiritual life, you may find it helpful to identify a spiritual director or spiritual companion. This is a person trained in assisting others to deepen their spirituality and who serves as a companion, providing feedback, guidance, and advice as you share the ups and downs and blessings and challenges of your spiritual journey. Typically, people meet with their spiritual director or spiritual companion monthly to check in, share spiritual insights, and discuss your spiritual experiences.

Help in identifying a spiritual director or spiritual companion can be provided by your local pastor or clergy person or the staff of your nearest retreat center. You may also want to consult a list of potential spiritual directors provided by Spiritual Directors International (SDI) using their website: https://www.sdicompanions.org/find-a-spiritual-director-companion/.

CHAPTER 9

CLOSING THOUGHTS ON AGING AND RETIREMENT

My hope for you in what I have written in the previous chapters is that you will see this next stage of life as a time not only to accept but to embrace growing older and to see retirement as a blessing and an opportunity to find new meaning and purpose in your life.

Our thinking and acting regarding where and how we find meaning and purpose in our lives can shift over time. Here are a few shifts commonly felt as we retire and continue to age:

- *From doing to being.* Being present in and enjoying life; being caring, being interested, being honest, being available, being truthful, being spiritual, and being involved with the important things in life. The focus changes from getting things done, with an emphasis on productivity and career success, to a more personal sense of simply being.
- *From saving to savoring.* Savoring everything—beauty in the arts and in nature, silence and solitude, and especially relationships. Wendy Lustbader has this insight on our relationships: "When closeness deepens with the passage of years, long-standing relationships become the bounty in later life." (Lustbader, *Life Gets Better: The Unexpected Pleasures of Growing Older*).

This transition from saving to savoring has been cleverly captured by E. B. White in "What Am I Living For?"

> *If the world were merely seductive, that would be easy.*
> *If it were merely challenging, that would be no problem.*
> *But I arise in the morning, torn between a desire*
> *to save the world and a desire to savor the world.*
> *That makes it hard to plan the day.*

- From career/professional practice to *becoming an elder.* Elderhood is characterized by a profound sense of perspective. Elders, often retired, have a unique understanding of life. They have experienced personal and societal changes and share the wisdom of those experiences.
- From being on a tight schedule to freedom of time and decisions—having freedom *to do what I want when I want, and some would add, with whom I want.* It is the transition from earning a living to making a life. The second half of life, for many of us, represents the first real chance we have had to define ourselves and to live in a manner of our own choosing, independent of our career and/or family responsibilities.
- From frenetic activity and impatience to get onto the next thing to *a more contemplative state,* recalling, relishing, and savoring those special moments in our lives.

So, as you continue on life's journey, I share with you the inspiring words of the poet Mary Oliver:

> One day you finally knew
> What you had to do, and began,
> Though the voices around you

Kept shouting Their bad advice,
Though the whole house
Began to tremble
And you felt the old tug
At your ankles. "Mend my life!"
Each voice cried.
But you didn't stop.
You knew what you had to do,
Though the wind pried
With its stiff fingers
At the very foundations,
Though their melancholy
Was terrible.
It was already late
Enough, and a wild night,
And the road full of fallen
Branches and stones.
But little by little,
As you left their voices behind,
The stars began to burn
Through the sheets of clouds,
And there was a new voice,
Which you slowly
Recognized as your own,
That kept you company
As you strode deeper and deeper
Into the world,
Determined to do
The only thing you could do,
Determined to save
The only life you could save.

ACKNOWLEDGMENTS

First, gratitude and appreciation to my wife, Kathy, to our four daughters—Elizabeth Briggs Farrell, Eileen Briggs Brinker, Jennifer Briggs Fisher, and Julie Briggs Dunn—and their four wonderful husbands, without whose encouragement and support, this book would not have been written. Even several of our older grandchildren were cheering me on!

I also want to thank my good friend Tom Bobich; my longtime career development colleague and friend Chris Shinkman; and our daughter Jennifer for their careful reading of my draft manuscripts. Their helpful copy editing and substantive comments and suggestions on the content of the book were invaluable to me.

Thanks, too, to Tom Bachhuber, founder and former executive director of the Center for Life Transitions, with whom I have conducted a number of retreats over the years. His encouragement and support are much appreciated. Gratitude also goes to all those who have worked in this field of career and life transitions and made a difference in the lives of so many people over the years.

I want to recognize especially my early mentors and supporters, both of whom are deceased—John Crystal of Crystal Management Services, who guided me through my first major life transition in my early thirties, and his colleague and my friend and neighbor Richard Bolles, author of *What Color is Your Parachute*. Both were instrumental in launching the start of my work in career counseling.

I also want to acknowledge the leadership of the Ignatian Legacy Fellows program, with whom I worked over the past few years in helping to develop and deliver the curriculum of this valuable program for soon-to-be retirees and recent retirees seeking to discern their future direction through the lens of Ignatian spirituality. Mariann McCorkle; Father Michael Garanzini, SJ; Joe DeFeo; and John Fontana, I am deeply grateful for the opportunity to work with you.

Finally, my gratitude to the staff of Covenant Books, who accepted this book for publication and provided the editorial support to move from manuscript to a beautifully designed book ready for publication and distribution. Special thanks to Ashley Matthews, my publication assistant.

My deep appreciation and gratitude to all!

Jim Briggs

FOOTNOTES / CITED RESOURCES

1. From the poem "The Summer Day" by Mary Oliver (House of Light, Resource Press, 1990).
2. John E. Nelson and Richard N. Bolles, *What Color Is Your Parachute for Retirement* (Ten Speed Press, 2010).
3. Institute on Aging (San Francisco, CA).
4. Richard Leider and David Shapiro, *Claiming Your Place at the Fire* (Berrett-Koehler, 2004).
5. Joan Chittister, *The Gift of Years: Growing Older Gracefully* (Blue Bridge, 2008 2014).
6. Wendy Lustbader, *Life Gets Better: The Unexpected Pleasures of Growing Older* (Penguin Group, 2011).
7. Parker Palmer, *On the Brink of Everything – Grace, Gravity, and Getting Old* (Berrett-Koehler Publishers Inc., 2018).
8. William Stafford, *The Way It Is* (Graywolf Publishing, 1999).
9. David Brooks, *The Second Mountain: The Quest for a Moral Life* (Random House, 2019).
10. Ron Rolheiser, *Sacred Fire* (Image, 2014).

BIBLIOGRAPHY

Top Resources and Reading Recommendations

Aronson, Louise. *Elderhood: Redefining Aging, Transforming Medicine, Reimagining Life.* Bloomsbury Publishing, 2019.

Au, Wilkie and Noreen Cannon. *Aging with Wisdom and Grace.* Paulist Press, 2019.

From a Christian perspective that deals with the opportunities and challenges that come with growing older, this book is a rich source of insight and practical help on the human journey into aging. The authors draw on their personal history as well as their theological and psychological depth.

Brooks, David. *The Second Mountain: The Quest for a Moral Life.* Random House. 2019.

This book is an inspiring and thought-provoking exploration of what it is to live a life of meaning and purpose. While deeply personal, it also offers a provocative social commentary on the current state of our society and culture. The first mountain we climb is focused on getting a good education, building our careers, and pursuing all those things our culture says we need to be happy and successful but find unsatisfying. The second mountain represents the journey from being self-centered (hyper-individualistic) to other-centered (relational) as the real way to self-fulfillment.

Chittister, Joan. *The Gift of Years: Growing Older Gracefully.* Blue Bridge, 2008, 2014.

This is a collection of inspirational reflections on the many facets of the aging process, from purposes and challenges to struggles and surprises. It is my first-choice recommendation for those seeking a better understanding of growing older. Full of insights on the new beginnings this stage of life can offer, each chapter ends with a summary of the burdens and blessings that go with the gift of aging.

Cowan, Rachel and Linda Thal. *Wise Aging: Living with Joy, Resilience, and Spirit.* Behrman House, 2015.

This book encourages us to see the new doors of opportunity that open to us with each year of life's journey, even while other doors close with loss. It provides insight and inspiration for welcoming the opportunities and navigating the challenges in ways that give new joy and meaning in life. Each chapter offers reflection questions and contemplative practices that help personalize the content.

Fleming, David. *Draw Me into Your Friendship: A Literal Translation and a Contemporary Reading of the Spiritual Exercises.* 2016.

Hansen, R. Jack and Jerry P. Haas. *Shaping a Life of Significance for Retirement.* Upper Room Books, 2010.

Johnson, Richard P. *Creating a Successful Retirement: Finding Peace and Purpose.* Liguori Publications, 1999.

Kelly, Matthew and Allen R. Hunt. *The Fourth Quarter of Your Life: Embracing What Matters Most.* Wellspring, 2022.

Leider, Richard and David Shapiro. *Claiming Your Place at the Fire.* Berrett-Koehler, 2004.

This book and its companion *Something to Live For – Finding Your Way in the Second Half of Life,* Berret-Koehler, 2008, focus on the journey of the second half of life and how we can clarify for ourselves what really matters in our lives, focusing on positive practices that help us live a life of purpose and meaning. The authors draw on the personal experiences of "eldering" they have experienced in their visits to Tanzania.

Lustbader, Wendy. *Life Gets Better: The Unexpected Pleasures of Growing Older.* Penguin Group, 2011.

This book offers insight, advice, and guidance for those growing older. The issues of aging are explored through first-person stories as well as the personal observations of Lustbader herself,

a former social worker and now a university professor special-
izing in aging. The central message is that there are discoveries
and pleasures in growing older, including self-knowledge and
increasing intellectual, emotional, and spiritual awareness.

Palmer, Parker. *On the Brink of Everything—Grace, Gravity, and Getting Old*. Berrett-Koehler Publishers, Inc., 2018.
This book is a collection of lessons gleaned from contemplating
one's life while aging. It is a helpful guide to aging reflectively,
seeking new insights and life-giving ways to engage the world.
He encourages us to regain our ability to convert suffering into
resurrection instead of fear. Warm, generous, and funny, Palmer
invites us to embrace our aging, where cultivating a vital inner
and outer life becomes a pressing concern.

Pevny, Ron. *Conscious Living, Conscious Aging—Embrace and Savor Your Next Chapter*. Atria Paperback, 2014.
This book explores different perspectives on aging and promotes
an empowering perspective on what aging can mean to individuals and to society—a time of continuing personal fulfillment
and spiritual growth. It offers helpful practices and exercises to
promote conscious aging.

Pipher, Mary. *Women Rowing North: Navigating Life's Currents as We Age*. Bloomsbury Publishing, 2019.
This book offers a timely examination of the cultural and
developmental issues women face as they age. Women growing older contend with ageism, misogyny, and loss. Yet most
older women are deeply happy and filled with gratitude for the
gifts of life. Their struggles help them grow into the authentic,
empathetic, and wise people they have always wanted to be.
The author, a cultural anthropologist and clinical psychologist,
offers wisdom, spirituality, and empathy for making the most
of this stage in life.

Reynolds, Chanel. *What Matters Most*. Harper Wave, 2019.
This book provides step-by-step practical advice on all the
details needing to be taken care of in advance of one's life taking a turn or the approach of one's death—relevant personal

information, advance medical directives, wills/estate planning, insurance, funeral plans, emergency fund, etc.

Rohr, Richard. *Falling Upward: A Spirituality for the Two Halves of Life*. Jossey Bass, 2011.

This book is dedicated to understanding the spiritual aspects of aging. It presents a paradigm for appreciating how our failings can be the foundation for ongoing spiritual growth in the second half of life as we find deeper meaning in our experiences. Rohr has a depth of thinking that at, times, I find challenging but rewarding if you stick with him.

Rolheiser, Ron. *Sacred Fire*. Image, 2014.

With a foundation in Christian spirituality, this book promotes spiritual awareness and maturity for those in their later years as we shift from a focus on ourselves to others. It encourages a deep intimacy with God, which in turn helps us give our lives away to others in more meaningful ways. Key concepts of gratitude, generativity, forgiveness, and blessing are explored through helpful new insights from scripture stories.

Singh, Kathleen Dowling. *The Grace in Aging*. Wisdom Publications, 2014.

This is a practical guide into the psycho-spiritual dynamics geared to the later stages of life. It focuses on how to awaken their promise and potential and "live in a more deeply sensed connection with the sacred." In allowing awakening to unfold, we can transform the predictable sufferings of aging into opportunities for growth in clarity, love, compassion, and peace.

Strosahl, Sally. *Loving Your Marriage in Retirement*. In the Round Publishing, 2018.

Taylor, Denise. *Rethinking Retirement for Positive Aging*. Routledge Publishing, 2024.

Zweig, Connie. *The Inner Work of Age—Shifting from Role to Soul*. Park Street Press, 2021.

Websites on Retirement and Aging

AARP.org (American Association of Retired Persons)

Alliance for Retired Americans (retiredamericans.org)

AROHR.org (Association of Retirement Organizations in Higher Education)

centerforconsciouseldering.com

Conscious Aging/Institute of Noetic Sciences (noetic.org)

eldersaction.net (Elders Action Network)

encore.org

fiercewithage.com

gratefulness.org

Institute of Contemporary Eldering (mepkinabbey.org/wordpress/ mepkin-abbey-institute-of-contemplative-eldering/)

lifereimagined.AARP.org

National Center for Creative Aging (creativeaging.org)

National Institute on Aging (NIA.NIH.org)

onbeing.org

retirementoptions.com

revolutionizeretirement.com

roadscholar.org

sageing.org

ABOUT THE AUTHOR

Jim Briggs has a background in higher education, theology, and career development. He is the retired Executive Director of the School of Applied Theology, where, from 2010 to 2015, he led the sabbatical program for people in need of rest, renewal, and rejuvenation. The demographic of this group was people in their sixties and seventies asking themselves what was next in their lives after their sabbatical. It was during this time with SAT that Jim, himself turning seventy, began his extensive reading on the subjects of aging and retirement planning. This, coupled with his experience in career counseling, led to the development of a course on discerning what's next in your life. This course then became the substance of the retreats and workshops Jim has been leading for the last ten years.

Jim's work in career development originated because of a major life transition of his own in the early 1970s. He transitioned from his ministry as a Catholic priest to his new lay role as a career/life counselor. During this time of transition, he was a client and protégé of John Crystal of Crystal Management Services. John had developed a program for reenvisioning one's life work, summarized in his book *Where Do I Go from Here with My Life*. John's program provided the foundation for Richard Bolles in writing his bestselling book *What Color Is Your Parachute*. Both men, now deceased, were instrumental in Jim's early work in career counseling, serving as Director of Career Planning and Placement at Georgetown University and the University of California–Berkeley.

Jim left UC–Berkeley in 1999 to serve for twenty-two years as vice president of Student Services and then Executive Assistant to the President at Santa Clara University.

Jim is married to Kathy Gannon-Briggs, his wife of fifty years. They have four daughters and sons-in-law and twelve grandchildren. He is currently "retired" but continues to offer workshops and retreats on retirement and conscious aging for those transitioning into their later years.

www.ingramcontent.com/pod-product-compliance
Lightning Source LLC
Chambersburg PA
CBHW031431130726
47989CB00003B/1087